Party like a Mock Star!

D1503028

Zoe Robinette

Mock Star®

Acknowledgements

Thank you to everyone involved in this project, from those who read it and said add more commas [add a comma here] to all the cheerleaders who rallied! Beverly Rivas thank you for being a part of this adventure from the onset. Thank you, Cynthia, for being an inspiration. Michelle Arbeau thanks a heap for urging me to write this book and making it all happen. A big thank you to Michael Davie for the many hours you spent sifting through these pages, working with me and for going the distance with *Party like a Mock Star!*

***

Library of Congress Cataloging-in-Publication Data

Copyright: Zoe Robinette 2016
Names: Robinette, Zoe, author.
Title: Party Like a Mock Star / Zoe Robinette
Description: Ancaster, Canada, Manor House, 2017
ISBN softcover: 978-1-988058-17-7
ISBN Hardcover: 978-1-988058-18-4
Subjects: Non-Fiction / Biography / BISAC:
BIO022000 Biography & Autobiography / Women;
CKB008000 Cooking / Beverages/ Non-Alcoholic;
SEL000000 SELF-HELP / General
Publisher: Manor House Publishing Inc. www.manor-house.ca (905-648-2193) in association with Authentic You Media, 2017
Printed in the United States of America
Cover Design: Tye Warner, Michael Davie
Interior layout-design-edit: Michael Davie
For more information visit: www.mockstar.tv

This Book is dedicated to Sissy and Bubby. I love you!

Table of Contents:

Preface

"Alcohol, because no great story ever started with someone eating a salad."
- anonymous

I will admit that I am a lightweight drinker. I have been a lightweight drinker since I was in my teens.

I fully accept making a mockery of myself in the process of sharing my drinking stories with you.

Although I was not any wilder than most of my friends, [actually, I tell some of their stories too] it just took me an exceptionally long time to figure out that alcohol does not mix with everything. That is correct, *just about* everything, but we can talk about all that later. All it took was an alcoholic drink or two.

What I finally had to do to save my sanity and my social grace, was to perfect the art of pretending to drink alcohol, while not taking a sip of the amazing brain altering nectar.

I never seemed to get around to using the mocking skills to save, rectify or breathe life into any of my love affairs, but there is another story altogether.

However, I used these mocking techniques while out with associates, and friends at various venues and functions without just settling for the cola in the soft drink glass. Yes, the art of mocking has been tested and proven.

What we are going to share in this little guide, are some of the party-until-you-drop antics and the final making of the original *Mock Star*!

Mocking in the traditional sense and the way it was used in such a hilarious way on *Saturday Night Live,* for any of you old enough to remember, the *"You Mock Me"* bits was making fun of someone or something in a derogatory manner. I still love the skits. They are classics.

We use the term differently in this girls' guide to *Party like a Mock Star!* Mock Stars are not contemptuous, sarcastic, disrespectful, or insulting. In no way is the term, meant to mock your many close friends, family, and associates who are consuming alcoholic beverages.

Mocking is artfully drinking a "Mocktail' to mimic drinking a real cocktail. I have finessed the art of mocking and have used it in countless situations and venues repeatedly, without as much as a sideways glance.

Well, sure there were times, when my sheer tendency to over indulge in Mocktails, had a few of my partying friends concerned that I may not be fit to drive myself home. I love my friends.

This is not a typical self-help book. This is a freaking virtual women's chat session that is exaggerated here and there for fun, of course!

This guide will show you how to take part in the dozens of events on your social calendar spiked with libations and entertainment and go home completely sober for a change.

This little guide will have hit its maker's mark if the stories sound vaguely familiar and you can laugh at your many past escapades, while you learn to mock your way through life with class, and self-confidence. A Mock Star is born!

1: Almost Everything Happens by Accident

"A beautiful lady is an accident of nature. A beautiful old lady is a work of art. "
- Louis Nizer

Everything in my life happens by accident, so I claim. Seriously, though, every accident that happened in my life started with a choice I made at some point.

Early on, I needed to be a rebel, slightly bad. Not bad enough to write a book about one-night stands, that is, unless you are looking for tips on one great piece of furniture that will look lovely by your bed.

This book escapade, for example, came about accidently, although it was a conscious choice to mock the event. I was very successfully having Mocktails at a friend's wedding, with my Mocker friend Bev. We discussed what it was we loved so much about drinking alcohol in the first place, aside from the obvious, which we will get into later.

I adore the stemware, in this order, the martini glass, the champagne flute, wine glass and a margarita glass. These glasses are the perfect design, not only for how they open the alcohol served in them, but also are fully intended to seduce the female drinker.

There is a lot of psychology around it, but you are not here for a shrink wrap, you are here for a Mocktail rap, so just know that guys are very keen on which glasses are specifically 'chick' glasses and most of the men I know avoid ordering those drinks because of the chick factor.

In an article, I read recently, Dave Danger head mixologist-bartender, at Kimoto Rooftop Beer Garden, in Brooklyn, says that most men will avoid ordering anything that is served in a martini glass, a coupe or a flute because that stemware is simply too girly for them to handle.

I have witnessed this first hand: Other men, and some women, heckle males when seen drinking cocktails typically supped on by the ladies. Men want to be men and according to Dave Danger, men prefer to hold something substantial in hand.

Women prefer to hold something substantial in hand as well, but that has nothing to do with drinking alcohol.

According to me, and Dave, women prefer to hold something sleek and sexy in hand. *Sex in the City* did a lot to push that hypothesis and make it stick. Back in the day, when advertisements showed women in sexy garments, only serving the martinis to men, those glasses were fine, three olives on the side.

However, things have changed and now women drink just as much as the men do.

My sister Mocker, Bev said she adored the garnish, the olives, lemon slices, and the stalk of celery in the morning after Bloody Mary, and last but not least, the umbrella.

I have to agree with Bev, the umbrella in the drink is a very cool girlie drink garnish. I have used the Mocktail umbrella drink successfully on many occasions.

At the wedding reception Bev and I attended, the idea to write a book for cocktail cuties and soon-to-be Mocktail converts was born.

This guide is for women who are sloshing their way through life one cocktail at a time.

You know this book is for you if you relate and have repeatedly related to states of intoxication labeled *slammed, hammered, lit, snockered, plastered, wrecked, three sheets to the wind, smashed, bombed, blitzed, tanked, totaled, sloshed, bashed, fucked up, plowed, toasted, juiced, trashed, twisted, wasted, stinko, under the table, soused, and stewed.*

The author of this book has used those terms copiously to describe various states of her own and her friends' inebriation. Let's face it none of those descriptors are glamorous, sexy, classy or socially acceptable.

This former cocktail cutie has been there, done that, and is going to vomit it all up for you in this tell-all guide.

Nevertheless, I will also pour out a few secrets to mindfully taking back your social grace using the Mocktail method.

Women of all ages, from the fake ID driver's license age, (*you know you had one*), the middle-aged socialite, whose calendar is overflowing with *must do* evening cocktail events, to the more mature woman, (*you know who you are*), should read this book.

This little tongue in cheek companion guide reveals what motivates women to drink, what they drink, and why it is just so darn plain easy to drink.

So, put down that glass of wine, because I'm going to give you tips on how to be social, refined and coherent for a change.

You will have an *absolutely fabulous* time out drinking with your friends, without the requisite hangover.

That's right – you are going to learn how to become a Mock Star.

2: You Get Your First Taste as a Kid

"Technically, you're not drinking alone if your kids are home" – anonymous

Friends asked me if I had a savings fund for my children's education. I told them no, I had some money stashed away for their professional counseling sessions.

I had my first Shirley Temple Mocktail as a kid; at age, five or six they get you started on your road to becoming a young, luscious-lush. They served me a very sweet little drink, with an umbrella in it too. Nearly everything I know about alcohol, I learned in grade school.

I ask you sober women, who in their right mind thought it was appropriate to dress up the kid like a mini-adult and order them their own 'cocktail'? We do not know whom to blame for that one, but we have a few suspects. Look, we're not truly blaming them, we're aware it took the edge off from mommy and daddy drinking martinis while out with the little buggers. Like most hooch history, no one can say who is responsible for the Shirley Temple drink. Staking claim to the classic cocktail is Chasen's Restaurant in Los Angeles, and the Royal Hawaiian Hotel, on Waikiki Beach also call dibs, but there are several liquor historians, that figure these assertions are not highly probable.

Ironically, the little starlet, Shirley Temple, herself, recalled at age 85, that the Brown Derby, in Los Angeles was the first place that she drank her namesake drink, with a maraschino cherry as garnish. The boys got their own version of the Shirley, called the Roy Rogers. Yep, sure they did, already separating alcoholic drinks by sexes.

Both of these drinks were around before most of us were born, and in the 1950s, the Shirley Temple, was one of the most popular drinks, at the top of the Mark in San Francisco. I love the Top of the Mark and have had my share of libations there, but they were more adult rated.

The umbrella in the drink still favors large in my enjoyment of it as a garnish, the maraschino cherry was never to my liking. Shirley admitted she never cared for the maraschino cherry either. It must be an acquired taste. Yet, that darling tiny umbrella tipped into the drink, elaborate and exotic, that was quite fancy. Who thought to put tiny umbrellas in the drinks in the first place? Ever sit around drinking a Mai Tai and ask yourself that question? Yeah, me too, so I looked it up. It seems that *how* tiny umbrellas became a cocktail garnish, has a colorful and not an exact historical account, according to those who are alcohol historians, like Dale DeGroff. He says that those mini umbrellas existed in China since 22AD. Therefore, it is a bit blurry as for how they play into the alcohol scene.

There is no proof perfect of who the original mastermind mixologist was with the eye for the fanciful fruity and exotic, although two bartenders are likely suspects according to our "boozeolgist", historians. One is the famous Harry Yee, who served it up at the Hilton Waikiki, in 1939, yet another is Don Beach, who had a bar chain called Don the Beachcomber. Some say he actually put the juice to the tiki umbrella drinks around 1959. He eventually sold out to Trader Vic.

Many have claimed that the original tiki joints used the garnishes to get more women into bars. The fruit forward mixologist, back in the day, along with mighty fine advertising, was just a way for men to get women into bars, saloons, booze halls, and voila, the tiki scene was born. *Women have been liberated and inebriated ever since.* One of my besties did the tiki scene, and before that, she worked at the famous Condor Club, during Carol Doda's infamous rise to salacious fame. My girl Connie, dishes out some juicy stories! Connie was a voice on the Blondie recording *"Hanging on the Telephone"* (we fast forward just to get to that part). Little things amuse us. We also loved watching the long-running television series, "Madmen." It brought back memories for both of us, although we were of slightly different eras.

Everyone can somehow relate to the perfectly coiffed Betty drinking at home, alone in the kitchen, while smoking a cigarette and pretty much ignoring the kids. Occasionally she would put on the evening gown and have drinks with Donald at a fabulous event, while the other entire cast of women on that series showed us how sexy it was to drink in the 1960s. They drank in the office at work, in the hotel suite for a noon liaison, and after work at a swank club, with the boss. It looked quite glamorous most of the time. That show truly reflected the times. I remember thinking how glamorous it was, as a kid watching the women in the neighborhood. Those were my lush-in-training years. I grew up in the exact same way as Betty's kids, taught by the best.

THE MOCKTAIL: The Shirley Temple

4 oz. lemon-lime mix
3 oz. 7-Up® soda
1 slice orange
1 maraschino cherry
3 - 5 drops grenadine syrup

Combine all ingredients into a Mocktail shaker with crushed ice and shake well. Pour it into a fancy glass on the rocks. Garnish with a slice of orange speared through a cocktail sword, tipped with a maraschino cherry.

3: It's a Family Affair

"If you cannot get rid of the family skeleton, you may as well make it dance." – George Bernard Shaw

I am not an alcoholic. I consider myself a lush, the distinction being that when I do drink (and sometimes there have been years between drinks), I often do not do it in moderation. In addition, modern research shows it is not all my fault.

"We are family, all my brothers and my sisters and me," right on Sister Sledge. Blame it on the family, all your issues and problems with alcohol; someone certainly is accountable for your behavior, and it may as not be you. There is science behind the ugly little fact that people are born with alcoholic genetic markers, so blame mom and dad, grandpa and grandma if it takes the edge off for you.

Yet, having a set of, *I-like-booze* chromosomes, does not mean that you will inevitably become an alcoholic. Nothing in life is that easy, you still have to work at it, practice daily and never stop.

I will wager you a bottle of Hiram, that there is at least one alcoholic in your family. We all have at least one.

Moreover, where there is one, there is a long lush line of alcoholics hanging on the branches of the family tree.

Probably both sides of the family tree – that's what keeps the tree from tipping over and uprooting. It's a balance thing.

I'm currently redoing my own family tree and replacing those little green leaves, with little martini glasses by all the appropriate names. I might come up with a co-dependent icon as well, to give the tree the color it needs.

My mom's family were the real corkers in the crowd, on my colorful family tree. They were of the Canadian whiskey brewing clan of the Walker varietal, drinking alcohol was a birthright to those people.

Drinking and singing Irish shanty songs – happy one minute, sobbing messes the next, they were a bunch that made for good story telling at least – although one never discusses such issues, with anyone outside of the family, it simply is taboo.

It's a family affair my dear and you take it to your grave with you when you kick it. That is how it is done in the old country and who are we to buck tradition?

THE MOCKTAIL: Canadian Tradition

2/3 oz. Canadian maple syrup

3 oz. grapefruit juice

3 oz. ginger ale

Fill glass ¾ full with broken ice. Add Canadian ginger ale, and garnish with a pretty slice of grapefruit.

Stemware: Collins Glass

When I kick it, I do not want a funeral. Do not bury me six feet under that would just kill me.

No, just let me fly free, let my ashes float away on the breeze off toward the water.

I definitely want one of my family's traditional booze it up after-funeral-parties sans the funeral.

After the funeral, parties are what we are talking about here. My cousins and I always amaze ourselves at how much fun we have, celebrating the life, of one of our deceased relatives.

Yet, at every after-funeral-party, eventually, someone would have a bit too much to drink and get a little out of hand, crying in their beer, telling everyone how much they love them or falling down a flight of one stair. I love my family.

One of the last funerals I attended was for my mother. I was the hostess to the after-funeral-party, at the family cottage. My mom's younger sister was 82-years-old and had pretty much stopped drinking by that time. I think her quitting had something to do with her health.

As I looked at her, I remembered the good old days, when that little blonde-haired woman, was always the life of the party. She lit up the room, just walking into it. Big smile, and dimpled cheeks, she made us all happy that she showed up to get the party started. She was our sophisticated, San Francisco cocktail cutie. She had the party scene down.

But there she sat now, prim, proper, sad and with the feeling most likely setting in that she was the last sister left to carry on.

I whispered in her ear *"how would you like a Sex on the Beach?"* She looked startled, and laughingly asked: *"well what's in it, honey?"*

I told her just booze. She smiled that classic smile and said *'bring me a double."* My cousin Billy wanted to throttle me.

THE MOCKTAIL: Safe Sex on the Beach

3 oz. cranberry juice
3 oz. grapefruit juice
2 oz. peach nectar
1 maraschino cherry

Pour it over ice into a chilled glass and stir, don't shake.
Garnish with a cherry.
Stemware: Highball Glass

Yet, she had to have a toast to Thelma, according to family tradition, and that's what it's all about.

Thelma was a corker and if anyone loved a good after-funeral-party, it was she, so it was fitting. I ended up writing mom's eulogy, to give her a proper send-off.

I added a little humor and well-intentioned stories, to help her friends and family remember the funny stuff, which always brings a tear.

And I did my best to tell the stories I could remember about Thelma, that I could actually repeat in front of a bunch of people.

Thelma was a women's rights advocate before that was a thing. One day, she decided to play in the all-male high school marching band and talked a friend into joining her scheme. They bobbed their hair, and broke into the historic all-male, marching band. That took some moxie.

I had to say that she loved being Irish. Let us not get into the fact that maybe she was – and maybe she was not – Irish. She loved to sing all the old Irish songs, I told my children. But I left out the part that she usually sang those down at The Doherty every night, hammered as one could get, with Aunt Edna, and then staggered on home and passed out.

I did say she liked to drink like the Irish and fight like the Irish, but if she loved you, she loved you with all her might. That was the truth about the woman. I failed to mention to my children, that if she held a grudge against you or was at odds with you, she took that to the grave with her. What they did not know would not hurt them.

So, driving with my children away from the cemetery burial spot – I swear to God we were still in the cemetery – I said to my kids: *Now listen, I do not want one of these funerals ever, you hear me? I want you to have a party amongst yourselves. I want you to spread my ashes into the wind, preferably near the river. If you have some family there, ok, but please tell some good stories. What were some of them thinking back there? I would appreciate it if you gave it some thought beforehand and came up with some damn good stories.*

My daughter Autumn, spoke up, *"Hey mom, why don't you just write down the stories you want us to tell when we do this letting-the-ashes-fly-into-the-wind thing and we will just read them ok?"*

My son added, *"Well, here's one of those stories right here."*

THE MOCKTAIL: Sweet Autumn

24 oz. canned apricot nectar
1 1/2 cups orange juice
3/4 cup lemon juice
1 1/2 quart sweet cider
20 maraschino cherries

Combine nectar, orange and lemon juices, and cider. Refrigerate until well chilled this apparently will serve a ton of after-funeral-party guests. Garnish with cherries or berries.

4: Booze 101

"A telephone survey says that 51 percent of college students drink until they pass out at least once a month. The other 49 percent didn't answer the phone."
- Craig Kilborn

Twenty-one is the legal age for drinking alcohol in the USA today. The operative word is *legal*, and *that word* is such a challenge to young adults.

Some cocktail cuties stumble into the intoxicating world of drinking booze before they have the legal right to *get hammered*. There has always been plenty of illegal swigging going on and most cocktail cuties had that pretty well nailed down by age 16.

There are a myriad of ways to get hooch, sauce, liquor, when you are underage, particularly if you are a young girl. My mother found me on hands and knees, barfing up my guts into the toilet when I was about that age. She leaned against the doorsill, all smug-like and laughed her haughty laugh, and before she strolled away, I heard her say, *"I guess that will teach you not to drink."* No, that taught me to switch to better booze. I started sneaking hers.

There are simply far too many drunken frat parties to mention. And besides, the movies *"Girls Gone Wild"* or *"Spring Break Babes"* pretty, much sum up college. We woke up to the smell of ganja wafting in through the window, every morning on campus, a fine way to start the day. A few co-eds tipped their way through every day; they may have been in the majority. I think that covers it.

We, co-ed babes, said drunken silly things when sloshed. I think girls are still saying the same things, with just a twist on vernacular.

Does any of this sound at all familiar to you girls?: *Yeah give me your number, let's do brunch tomorrow; OMG this is my song (every song is my song). Holy shit, I am totally wasted, yeah I want another one. Why did I wear these stupid shoes tonight? OK, I am taking these stupid shoes off now. Shut Up! Seriously, just shut up for a second, this is important shit. I cannot believe he is here this was our place. Should I just leave? I cannot believe she is here, how dare she kill my buzz. OMG, we were just talking about you! Are you seriously sleeping right now? Dude, I am going to call him right now. Maybe he didn't get my message. Do you think he will call me? Wonder why he hasn't called? Do you think he lost my number? Men, I love em, just love em. Men, they just get on my last nerve. You are right, love sucks. You think he has another girl already. You intimidate him. He just can't handle you; you are so beautiful. You give him all the wrong vibes. I saw it, I was there, no, I am so serious; it was her. Give me my phone back now. I am going to text him right now. If he calls, I am not picking up. If he texts me should, I reply. Do you think I should go over and talk to him? Hey, get a load of that one over there. No don't look, don't look, oh damn you looked. No, trust me I am not that drunk. Where are we going after? Who wants a strawberry banana pie right now? Whoa, my face feels numb. Dude, you just spilled your drink all over me. I think I'm going to hurl. If I hadn't mixed those, two drinks like that, I wouldn't feel so sock, I mean sick. Sooooooo, sorry I barfed in your car. Do you hate me now? You are seriously my best friend. I totally love you. What? We were not talking that loud! I am totally going to get his number. Maybe I should go over and ask him to dance. Did Jill leave? If my mom asks, remember I stayed at your house because I already told her that. No, you look us. This place is lame. Let's just scoot across to r. I never-ever get caught. There's a cop, just act normal. Turn up the radio, this is my song. Do you know where we are? Are you sure, you can drive? I never get lost. I lost my purse. I lost my phone. I lost my keys. I lost my car. This was the best night ever!*

THE MOCKTAIL: Bloody Shame

3 oz. V8® vegetable juice
2-3 drops Tabasco® sauce – maybe more
1 pinch salt
1 pinch peppers
1 celery stick – or two

Pour V8 into an old-fashioned glass, add tabasco sauce and stir with a celery stalk. Sprinkle with salt and pepper, and serve. The celery stalk makes it!

Stemware: Rocks Glass

Talking about my generation, we burned our bras, let our hair go wild and free, tripped our butts off, did ludes, wore far out clothing and platform shoes and we drank. We acted out in ways to blow the minds of the older generation, the warmongers, and the capitalistic pigs, otherwise known as the establishment. Don't trust anyone over thirty was the code to live by and we meant it. Those were my college days, as best as I can recall.

We were peace loving, anti-establishment, sit-in *"make love, not war,"* pot-smoking, meth-taking, tripping, drinking people. Right on, far out, and heavy. That's what it was. All of our social brainwashing and training went up in smoke.

Today, girls are getting everything pierced or tattooed; rings are sticking out of a ton of different body parts. They color their hair blue, pink, green, which is one new look I adore, most of the time. When asking: "do these pants make my butt look big," they are now, actually looking for an affirmative reply.

They talk a little jive talk, but when you actually sit and talk with them and by them, I mean those under 30, they can be such sweet young women. When you tell them, you like their purple hair or ask them about their tattoo and what is symbolizes for them, they light up, talk, and share. At that moment, they are who they really are, at least for that period in their lives.

They just have new ways of acting out, in ways to blow the minds of the establishment, meaning the old hippies, who are now nearly ready to retire. All the social brainwashing they got, to be authentic, to follow their spiritual paths, to be free and to let themselves in after school, the key was under the mat, microwave food was in the freezer, kind of free.

Imagine how many ways, they heard that hippie-speak, or the Gen-X stuff. While they watch the destruction of the planet, through human disposable consumption, they only want it to stop. They are sick and tired of the war, the unrest all over the world, the stress of performing for whoever has them under their thumb at home, school or work. They just, honestly, want to do it their way. Save the planet, save humanity, hear their own music, do their own dance and shake some sense into the older generation. It's the same story, different decade, new generation.

My generation was kick ass! There is no doubt in anyone's mind, we were the generation to take charge, and change everything imaginable. Does every generation

21

stake that claim?   Probably, but talking about my generation:

"It's like gambling somehow. You go out for a night of drinking and you don't know where you're going to end up the next day. It could work out good or it could be disastrous. It's like the throw of the dice."~ Jim Morrison

One day hanging around campus in the square waiting for a friend to walk back to the dorm, an old van pulled up and stopped. When the dude rolled down the window a ton of purple smoke rolled out just like in a movie. The guy yelled, *"Hi there can you tell me where Williams Hall is, man?"* I recognized that Chicano voice, so I strolled over to the van to check it out. It was Cheech and Chong, slated to do a show on campus that night. *"Far out"*, I said trying to maintain my cool vibe. *"I can't believe I am meeting the famous Cheech and Chong! I dig your stuff man!"*

Wow, they said acting all impressed that anyone on the planet would recognize them, they got into their antics and cracked me up! I told them where the hall was and they gave me three backstage passes, one for me and two for my friends. That was a big kick! So there we were all dressed up in our coolest hot pants, crop tops and lace-up boots, hair all fro'd out just right with little skull caps on; the gaudiest of eye make-up, of course, but we knew we were looking fine.

The guys were cool and said we'd hang out after the show. Who dreamed the show was going to be cut short as hell? They were doing their tie-dyed tampon routine and some other raunchy stuff, their class act bits when the university decided that the students had seen enough and pulled their mic. Just as someone scrambled and got the mic plugged back in the last thing we heard was Chong yelling *"this isn't a university this is a fucking prison man!"* We were freaking out backstage and of course, the drinking and pot smoking didn't do a lot to help calm us down. The next thing you know we were in the van on the country roads smoking doobies with Cheech and Chong. We all thought their vinyl record albums were hysterical and sat around the dorm listening to them all the time. Meeting them and having all that shit hit the fan was pretty much the highlight of that semester. Years later in San Francisco at a Mexican Museum Art Installation, while in casual conversation with Cheech, I asked him if he remembered the night, he and Chong was kicked off stage at a University in Michigan. He just looked at me like, *what's up with you, did you just drop a hit of acid?*, and said laughingly, *"well not one, in particular, they kicked us off stage, almost every place we played, man."*

THE MOCKTAIL: Acapulco Gold

3 oz. pineapple juice
1 oz. coconut cream
1 oz. whipping cream
1/2 oz. grapefruit juice

Shake and strain into a highball glass with cracked ice

Did they also call my generation the ME generation? I cannot remember.

On a more current note, I sleuthed around to sift out the reasons young women drink alcohol today, to see if women are getting hammered for reasons other than we did. The answers have not changed much in all these decades.

The reasons have not changed, the only real difference in each decade, is that girls are getting blitzed using slightly different *methods*. Today, more binge drinking is going on, than ever before, yet the reasons have not changed.

Girls drink to fit in, to be popular, to be rebellious, to feel more comfortable around everyone, to cope with pressures to do well, to look grown-up, to act sophisticated, to come to understand their own sexuality, to make-believe they are glamorous, sexy and fun.

They also drink because of sadness, loss, grief and confusion that are all part of purely trying to grow up.

There is not a single-family structure or socio-economic status that plays an overriding factor in the reason *"that girls gone wild"* has *"gone wilder"* than ever before. The fact is, it's always been tough to grow up, in a world that is projecting so many false, photo-enhanced images, of what makes a girl pretty, unique and socially acceptable.

Today, these sexy girl images are bombarding chicks at the speed of light, and targeting even younger women from every angle. It's no longer just *Seventeen Magazine*® and a few ads. It's a 24- hour non-stop blitz. We've all been there, and while my generation was the catalyst for women's sexual and social liberation and the ever-popular inebriation, we did not realize just how far it would go, or that it would get this tipped.

The glam factor related to drinking booze progressively ramped up, hyped up, and consequently very young women today, have far greater pressure than my generation ever did. Yet, the reasons girls cite for drinking to excess, are the same reasons we mentioned, so many decades before. Same old song, heavier bass line, I think.

No matter what era in which we live, the same maturation process must occur. Mocking can be helpful for all the young and tween-age years and beyond. My dream for young women, everywhere, is for Mocking to go viral or become the rage. Whatever word is currently in vogue, to mean widespread, outrageously attractive, the new normal, whatever normal is, the *Mock Star revolution!*

5: Where Have All My Brain Cells Gone?

You know what I always say, booze kills brain cells, but I am not completely stupid yet!

Seriously, if booze actually killed brain cells, there are many women I know, who would be certifiably brain dead by this time. Actually, alcohol just messes with your brain. So, let's just say many of us have messed with our brains, from time to time.

Honestly, if booze does not kill your brain cells, I swear giving birth does. Just the giving birth part, the rest I loved. Although, when my kids were little, I used to wonder if I had misplaced my brain, as I'd misplaced everything else – the keys to the car, for example, were often later found in the refrigerator.

The kids freaked when we went to a mall, because nine out of ten times, I lost my keys in the mall somewhere. It took us an eternity of frantic fretting to find them. My son finally became the official key-carrier, when in a store of any kind. Where did that one sock go? What do you mean I forgot to pack your lunch? Who knew your spring break didn't start today? I am sorry kids. Just consider it an extra day off. Also, for some odd reason, I'd often call my son Duggie; that was our dog's name. In my defense, that was due, in part, to Duggie and Tye constantly going at it, chasing one another around. Tye says he still has nightmares about that dog.

However, moms today have amped up the volume. They are over the top! They make our little wine and cheese parties look like child's play, nothing but out-played, old school beginners. These young moms are full-on partying, what is left of their brains, out.

In New York's Westchester County, where I once hung my hat in a halfway respectful manner, moms are now passing around flasks at their kid's school functions. This ugly reality is mimicking reality television, real life, *"Mothers Gone Wild*!*"* playing soon in a neighborhood near you. Motherhood is now just one more excuse to get shit faced, blotto, hammered, turnt and lit. Talk about bottle-feeding.

The staggering number of female drinkers is at an all-time high! All the encouragement they need to get loaded is glaring at them from thousands of media sources, I call brain drain outlets. Moms' sporting t-shirts that read, *"Not so loud, I had book club last night."* I am not a fan of any t-shirt that has words on it. I would have to snub that one, just saying. *Moms Who Need Wine,* a social networking group on Facebook, has nearly 700,000 followers. When do they find the time? Another wine touting group, called *"OMG, I So Need a Glass of Wine or I'm Gonna Sell My Kids"* has a couple hundred thousand following them online. I am not a fan of that group either, on so many levels. However, remember girls, what goes around comes around. One day, these young hot moms will be older and greeted by their children wearing t-shirts that read, *"WTF, I So Need a Shot of Whiskey or I'm Gonna Sell My Mom."* The drinking mom has become as common, if not more widespread, as the drinking dad! Indeed, they have simply become common, in far too many ways, if you know what I mean, darling.

So common in fact, that nearly 800-million gallons of wine sell to women buyers, in the U.S. annually, meaning yearly, as in every 365 days, 800-million gallons of wine are being poured and guzzled on, in the grand old USA, according to recent wine distribution reports. There is lots of speculation, that many of the women purchasing, actually drink the wine, as well.   Let us break it down shall we? Yes, 800,000,000 gallons a year, is only about 2-million gallons a day, right.   I am not a mathematics wizard, but I am sure that it comes out to roughly 2,191,780.82 gallons of wine a day. Check my math. Yet, approximately 2-million gallons a day is not that big a load in a day, is it? The study did not say precisely, how many women were purchasing said wine daily. Could be a handful of women in the boozy states or maybe just a widespread trend in wine, *impulse buying*.

At my local grocery, the wine is conveniently located near the checkout stand, which always is helpful. Those lovely displays and snazzy little butler type gizmos that hold the cheese, paired specifically with that particular wine, are right there, so you can sample; not the wine, just the cheese. You nosh a little of the cheese and realize it is tasty; you decide to put the cheese in the cart. What a shame if you didn't have wine to go along with the cheese. They have a special price deal if you buy two bottles. What the heck, it would be insane not to grab a couple of bottles. Just in time, you notice, a case is actually a better deal. Tossing the toothpick into the little pouch on the cheese gizmo, you quickly put the two bottles back.

You ask the person at the checkout counter, if someone could lug that case of the wine, you have never tasted, to your automobile. Actually, quite thoughtful on the part of the grocer, you know how busy we women get, how forgetful we can be at times, we might walk right out of the store, without picking up a few bottles and have to turn around and run back for it later. Thankfully, there it was, right on your way out. Good, because you just have to get to the school on time to pick up the kids. They hate it when you are late and they have to sit on the steps, waiting for you, puts them in a mood. Moms, your kids have a way of growing up and are in high school before you can say,

Jack Daniels.   When mine did, I worried a little about them drinking. My kids are, how you say, gifted on both sides of the family tree, from a well-established alcoholic gene pool. Sorry kids, it is not entirely my fault.

I did not have drinks around them. I did not have alcohol at the house. I never drank alone. Never drank to excess if I went out. I felt I kept them pretty darn busy in sports and after school activities.

As they began high school, I bought a new house, with a huge backyard, on a beautiful boulevard. It was a hot, muggy summer day, as we unpacked and settled into our place. The kids took off on their bikes to see friends. I took the fold up chaise lounge, out onto my rickety deck, to catch a few rays and unwind, in my new backyard. I had not any more than plopped down for a nice little rest, when the chair went crashing through the deck, with me in it! All the neighbors who were also out in their backyards, minding their own business, got a load of the new neighbor, falling through her deck, laughing hysterically at that top of her lungs, unable to lift her bikini-clad bottom, up out of the chair to get back onto the deck.

Falling through your deck, laughing until you nearly pee your pants, laughing until you can't move, I discovered is the best darn way to make friends and influence people. Everybody came running over and dragged me up and out of my precarious perch. Of course, being neighborly, they brought beer and offered me a cold one. I hated beer, but I wanted to be neighborly, so I sloshed it down with them, all of us still laughing about the hole I had left in the deck. I knew right then, that this was going to be a fun neighborhood. That day turned on my lush light. I think Deadric Malone or somebody wrote a song about it *"Turn on Your Lush Light,"* whatever, I was beaming. I reached for the wine. The wine went with everything and everything went with wine. I would meet some of my girls at the club, at 5:05, to have wine and try very hard not to whine. Which was not easy, we all were working single mothers, wearing big executive hats, so whining was almost a given. In fact, the nights turned into wine-soaked bitching therapy sessions. Big buzz kill, so we made up a rule. If anyone bitched about their job, their kids, their boss or boyfriend, they had to throw a five-dollar bill on the table. Most nights the kitty did not get too high and we drank the kitty. One night, one of our friends came in, grabbed her usual spot at the table, threw down a twenty-dollar bill and hissed, *"Listen up bitches this has been the day from hell"* we let her vent and then bought a bottle.

Despite all of our various after school activities, we would gather at home for our family dinner hour. On the nights I planned to go out after work with friends, I usually made one of my memorable crock pot meals. Ok, every night, I made crock pot meals in those days. I could turn any dish, into a crock pot slow-cooked dinner. I was the Martha Stewart of crock pot cookery; had all the slow cooker cookbooks, an entire library.

Of course, my girl, my darling daughter would always know if I had stopped for a glass or two of wine. She would inquire in her cute, sly and incredibly perceptive way *"Have a little wine with your friends tonight mom?"* No, I lied while leaning against the doorjamb for support. Why do you ask?

THE MOCKTAIL: Virgin Peachino

2 oz. peach juice
1 tsp grenadine syrup
2 oz. soda water

Pour it into a big wine glass, and drink, repeatedly.
Serve in: White Wine Glass

6: Does This Wine Make Me Look Fat?

"Clear alcohol is for rich women on diets."
- The Office

I would love to meet a wine that kills fat cells and enhances brain cells. Hello, is anyone home? Our popular, Lisa Vanderpump, has a low-calorie wine, yet we want calorie free please, but I guess that would just be grape juice! By the way, and just for the record sweetie, *free wine* still has the same amount of calories! No one ever said life was fair. My best gal pal Wendy and I would have our regular country club business lunches, which ran on into most of the afternoon, complete with at least one bottle of wine.

Wendy worked for a wine distribution company! What a friend! Be still my wino's heart. If I were going to be a full-on alcoholic, I would definitely be a wino. My friend Wendy and I had some superb wine on our outings, to test for her business, of course. Our body weight combined was about 200 pounds. A woman weighing in at around 100 pounds can consume roughly a thimble full of liquor before she is snockered. We would start with the wine and forgo the food as we were constantly on a diet. As my dear friend, Wendy always said: *"Honey, if we have to give up calories, let's not eat food!"* Cheers to us girlfriend! Actually, we were so ahead of our time, as usual. There is now, an entire diet craze around that very concept, we so aptly adopted back in the day. Wendy and I were all together and perhaps a little boozy, on those afternoons, but it worked for us.

There is a wild new diet, sort of a spin-off from our original diet plan, on campus today, *Drunkorexia.* Lindsey Hall, who I read about in a recent article, claims it was the way for her to stay slim, had the extra co-ed benefits of getting in studying time, while partying as well. Lindsey was one heck of a multi-tasker. A co-ed who almost had it all worked out. Although Wendy and I had not taken it quite this far, we were on the cutting edge, we practically invented this foolishness, although we were quite chic at the time. As she mentioned just the other day, *"we were always trendsetters honey."*

Drunkorexia is a street term, simply meaning, barely eating, as in maybe tossing down a tick-tac for a meal and then just drinking, until full, trashed, buzzed, blitzed, fried, sloshed, shit-faced full in fact. Lindsey, who is now 27, said she'd forego eating food so she could have her drinks and maintain her weight when she was in college. Lindsey and a self-reported one-third of all college girls use this *liquid booze diet* method to stay slim. The same way Wendy, almost every chick and I did. Add a cigarette and you wouldn't be hungry for days. *As they say, you can never be too rich or too thin. You can be too drunk, however!* That's where this whole *Drunkorexia* diet scheme runs amuck.

Drunkorexia is a not well thought out, coping mechanism, to stay thin, to fit in, to drink just like everyone body else, to handle stress, college, grief, sex, competition, and life, in general. A couple of glasses of wine, half a bottle and you are no longer hungry. While *Drunkorexia* has taken the Wendy and Zoe methods over the top, it is something that could lead them to plenty of snockered up trouble and some health issues actually. We had our share of smallish issues, and there was a time or two when the Wendy diet method backfired. One was at a wedding, her husband the Reverend Mr. Wendy was officiating. She wore a sleek

31

Chanel off-white dress and Gucci heels. She loved red wine and unlike me, she could actually drink wine without spilling it all over the front of whatever she was wearing. I idolized the woman. Yet, on this particular occasion, which I was not there to witness, she told me she got a tad bit tipsy and tipped into one of the big red wine fountains. She said she went in ass first, spread eagle, into the vino bin, heels up. I know her hubby adored her and most likely laughed while helping her out of that vat. I adored her too and was bummed I had missed that graceful move.

Actually, I wished I could drink red wine, without wearing it. I generally spilled the red wine on my left breast. Wendy's theologian husband took that particular placement of incessant spilling, as a sign of the sacred heart, the blessed one. The bunch of us had so much fun together, drinking the nectar of the holy ones.

The three of us would drink wine in the hot tub, at the ski hill, at every function in town and of course at our lunch hours away from work. The three-martini lunch was out, but no one mentioned wine, so it seemed like fair game.

Seriously, Wendy and I had quite a few adventures and most if not all of them included wine, of course. We would work out and then stop by the club, for a glass of wine. We would do a morning jog, followed by an afternoon of taste-testing wine. Her company health fair is the only one in the hundreds that I have participated in, that actually had a big Budweiser® Truck at the event with both beer and wine on tap for the gig, now that's a health fair! Did we drink and drive? I would say maybe. Yet, most places were within walking distance or we had a driver. Drivers definitely come in handy.

Wendy and I were very excited for my son, when he got his first automobile, and not for the sole purpose of having a *driver*. So we grabbed our glasses of wine and the bottle and hopped in the backseat and said in accent, the only one we had, *'drive James'*

We did not go two miles when a police c over for God knows what. Tye gave us a wicked ⌐ in the rear view mirror and handed the nice policeman ⊓⌐ driver's license and proof of insurance.

The officer looked into the backseat and said sarcastically, *"Well, ladies are you trying to get this young man in trouble?"* Well no, we were just celebrating his new automobile we said, all smiles and flirty, like that was going to help. I'm sure he knew I was the District Judge's honey and that Wendy was married to a minister.

He looked back at Tye *"you can go now, but don't ever let anyone have open alcohol in your automobile again. Next time it's on you."* Wendy and I were giggling in the back seat. Tye drove us back to my house and dumped us off without uttering a word.

THE MOCKTAIL: My-Tye

Mock Mai Tai
3 ounces fresh orange juice — ¾ 6 oz = ¾ cup
Juice of 1/2 fresh lime
1 teaspoon fine sugar
1 tablespoon of almond syrup —
½ ounce grenadine — 1 Tablespoon
Add crushed ice
Shake it up

Combine all ingredients except crushed ice in a Mocktail shaker half-filled with ice. Shake well, until it gets a little cool on the outside. Strain into a highball glass half-filled with crushed ice. Garnish with a slice of fruit and a tiny darling drink umbrella. *You can drink this one in the car.*

7: Glam Shots

"Pour yourself a drink, put on some lipstick and pull yourself together."
- Elizabeth Taylor

What kills me is how glamorous they make drinking look in commercials and in magazines. Always first class, fun, vivacious, gorgeous people drinking, laughing, flirting and enjoying the best that life has to offer. There are clearly different types of glamor, for each target audience and it does not take much market research, to figure out what is going to sell. Sex sells.

The wild 1960s, when women were coming of age, frequenting tiki bars, swooning over the Beatles, wearing mini-skirts and going *"007 Bond Girl"* sexy, got a big boost through media hype, movies, commercials and just absolutely fabulous ads from the Madison Avenue gurus and the California wine growers.

First Lady, Jacqueline Kennedy, invited 56-million viewers on tour through the white house in 1962. Jackie was glamorous, the first political wife celebrity icon, she set the bar. Seriously, she *did* set the *bar* and had her fabulous crystal stemware next to each place setting. Big hit with the ladies, drinking wine was suddenly vogue. Thanks to Jackie, the manufacturer of that stemware said they could barely keep up with orders after that documentary aired. That wasn't impulse buying. That was from the white house to my house, I too am glamorous.

Imagine just how talented the ad people have to be to land a booze campaign. Who is in charge of alcohol campaigns? Alcohol is a product that everyone wants. It has been since the World *"Part Un."* There is no question. Everyone is going to buy.

They have to dream up and kick off the most alluring advertising blitz, in the business, to steer the herd in their brand's direction. If their pitch does not have the juice, the consumers will buy from the millions of other brands out there.

The actors and models used to shoot the ads, billboards, and the commercials, cast to perfection. Cheers to you, the casting directors! The stylists on set are professionals and create flawless beauty on those faces. Now that is glamor. Ask yourself how many clubs, social events, and venues you have attended that every person there was drop dead gorgeous including the wait staff. *In Los Angeles, almost all of them, it is true.*

Moving on, how often has every woman in the place had the perfect make-up, coiffure and ensemble, posing in the most elegant and seductive way and the same with the men for that matter? How many look that way after drinking a few hours? How many with the perfect make-up artistry still looks perfect cocktail after cocktail, hour after hour without their personal makeup artist retouching their blotched up faces. How many dazzling smiles still have that dazzle after one too many rounds?

Seriously, as gorgeous as you are, I know you have seen pictures of yourself after drinking a bit too much. I know you have immediately deleted them.

But trust me, one of your friends has that picture of you and you know she is going to post it to Facebook like *"we had so much fun last night"* you will want to immediately click delete, but that would make you look worse than the photo! So you laugh at yourself *"LOL, yeah what a blast!"* It is not a coincidence that the paparazzi captures beautiful women celebrities looking a bit looped – because they *are* looped.

Paparazzi, hover, morning, noon and night and catch their glamorous drunken episodes on film, repeatedly. Then, of course, they publish those *'becoming'* photos all over the world. These women are celebrity enough to get their real DUI mug shots plastered all over the news. Glam shot morphs to Mug shot.

My issue was that when I saw those wine glasses, sultry martini glasses, sexy champagne flutes or those rocking Margaretta glasses, I wanted to party. I wanted to hold one of those and look like the advertisements that went with the intoxicating magic, they were hawking.

I was no different than the millions of women, who went out and bought the beautiful crystal stemware, just like Jackie Kennedy. It's so *"Sex in the City"* on our part, to strut our stuff into the local club, with our crew. Now *that* is glam. Let's all take a shot!

MOCKTAIL: Faux Cosmopolitan

Organic Cranberry Juice
7 Up® or Sprite® or a Lemon-Lime Soda
Dash of Grenadine
Twist of Lime
Dip the rim of the martini glass in sugar and garnish with a slice of lime. Drink responsibility-drink faux cosmos!
Stemware: Sexy Martini Glass

8: Everything is Political

"My makeup wasn't smeared. I wasn't disheveled, I behaved politely, and I never finished off a bottle, so how could I be an alcoholic"
- Betty Ford

Everything is political ladies, everything. Welcome to the world, *"part tois"* everyone has an agenda. The difference is you have a relatively decent blueprint of everyone's agenda in a political battle. Not so in the corporate setting, people's agendas sneak up on you and stab you in the back when you've turned to walk away. So in that sense, you have better odds of knowing who the players are and what they are after in the political arena.

Yet politics itself is a voracious whore. I should know, I started in high school working on Mr. Meek's bid for state congress. I did my share of stumping the campaign trails throughout my life. And I can tell you first hand that there is a whole lot of drinking going on, stumbling your way down the campaign trail.

And it's not just the politicians and their entourage who get tanked. I once said that many of the politicians' wives are alcoholics and for a good reason. Think about it. The wife has to wear the right clothing, have the perfect coiffure, know the right people, or have the ability to open that door, say the correct things and smile at everyone, regardless of how she feels. If she is secretly pro-choice and her political husband is on the pro-life bandwagon, she has to keep her mouth shut.

She has to smile, while he's schmoozing with men and women, every minute, of every event. She has to listen to him tell the same lame jokes and stories event after event. She has to do his bidding, to get that coveted seat next to the senator or at the governor's table and she knows exactly how to do that. She has to learn the art of saying what she is expected to say, without saying much at all.

When he gets elected she has to continue in her role, mask her emotions, make believe and hide her feelings and her identity as a person. She isn't a person any longer, she's an accessory. She has a part but it's a bit part. She has to hide someplace. She hides in the bottle.

I do have to tip my hat to Hillary Clinton. I may not agree with her on everything, but she is one hell of a woman. She handled her marriage to Bill, for that alone we stand in awe. She handled her role as a servant to the nation for her entire professional career. She handled a seat on the Senate. She handled her role as Secretary of State. She handled her debates with Trump with as much class as she could, given the circumstances. She handled being the first woman to run for President of the USA. What there's to be said about Hillary is: *she can handle it*. I am not sure if she drinks alcohol, but at her age, she should consider Mocking – not sure she can handle booze, entirely – but I'm speculating.

Trump, on the other hand, ran his campaign like a man whose mind was still in the 1960s. Do you think he had a couple of shots before he took to the stage? Do you think he was totally blitzed tweeting at 3:00 am? I do. Others say he was just 'coked up' I believe that it was Princess Laya who said that first, but then thought about it twice and could not decide if he had gone to the dark side or not.

The Trump campaign made the Palin fiasco look almost sane. Palin stuck to the GOP like gum to the bottom of their shoe, just so tough to get rid of, that gum. Talk about drinking and politics, Palin lowered the bar, and I mean that in every sense of the word, with her juiced up escapades. Politics, is a mind-numbing experience, particularly the 2016 campaign season, which in my humble and sober opinion, will change the electoral process in America forever. I think Americans have indeed been living in the land of Oz and finally saw the curtain drawn back to get a load of the Great and Powerful Wizard. Thank you Toto, I mean Donald.

Instead of corporate America sitting in the back seat of the limo, telling the government which turns and lane-changes to make, we're witnessing corporate America, sitting in the driver's seat, with a buddy riding shotgun and friends in the backseat partying it up, drinking vodka, and joy riding. There's speculation that the entire nation is contemplating going on a major bender... *America the land of the free is now more than ever, the home of the brave.*

I've cavorted with many a politician with the wife-in-the-bag in my day. I've navigated my way around invitations from sleazy politicians. I've shrugged off totally inappropriate sexual remarks by politicians, pundits, and constituents, back in my young stumping days. *Women, you must have a strong constitution, to get into politics.*

Now that Donald, the accused and self-reported woman groper, is the 45th President of the USA, we should all fasten our seat belts, for we are in for a bumpy ride Pilgrims. I imagine him on the phone swapping locker room stories with Putin. We have been schooled, on how well all the good old boys would take to a woman with her hands on the wheel, driving that much horsepower, during the campaign season of 2016. Despite the passing years, men still like to be on top, in so many ways.

THE MOCKTAIL: The Bernie (honoring Bernie Sanders)
Fresh grapefruit juice
A splash of fresh lemon juice
Ginger beer
Cherry juice
Fresh rosemary
Shake it up and top it off with ginger beer
Add grapefruit drizzled over it if you want along with a swig of rosemary for garnish.
Stemware: Fluted Champagne Glass

Some of us had hoped Bernie would shake it up a bit more in 2016, but overall, Bernie didn't stir things up too much. Mixologist Vincent Hale, who deserves to take a bow, constructed the Bernie Mocktail! I made one at home and loved it! I did feel the Bern in a good way!

I am partial to former First Lady, Betty Ford though and even have official Betty Ford Center logoed items, the golf sun visor and a set of shot glasses, I think. I love that famous photo of her dancing on the table in the White House, thank you, Betty!

Like Betty, I was a dancer-thespian, who got involved with a politician from the Great Lakes State of Michigan. I found me an Irish alcoholic politician, what luck. He had been divorced for a while and had quite the reputation all over the state as an asshole, skirt chaser. Now there is a new twist in the political world! Yet, I won his heart and his mind, and as you know, *winning* ranks high with politicians, co-dependents, and thespians. On a typical winter day in Michigan, below freezing temperatures, gray sky above, snow to the edge of the windowsill, the judge told me he had decided to run for Appellate Court. He asked if I thought our relationship could handle it, said it would be tough. At the time, I knew I could handle anything, let's just get this party started. We got out the bottle of B & B and sat in the hot tub to write his first campaign speech. It was a doozy. It truly was a winner and it stuck. We stumped all over Michigan with that very speech, making minor adjustments to it, depending on the audience we were playing to, it was theater after all. It was quite dramatic. Thespians and co-dependents love drama – they literally thrive on it in so many messed up ways.

Drama is probably the best word in the English language, for political life. It is the theater, the circus coming to town. Drama and intrigue, politics has everything any addictive personality type would love. *"I heard he takes drugs. He did have that girl from Lansing knocked up I hear. No, I hear he has three illegitimate babies, with three different women, all at the same time I tell you."* The political counter is to deny. My guy hammered the use of denial into my brain. *"Deny,"* he said, *"always deny, deny"* and that was in the event I ever got stopped speeding. They all have that certain something they do not want the world to know and will deny it up to and sometimes, including perjury if need be. The alcoholic dynamic is no different. They deny they have a drinking problem until – *and sometimes even after* – being forced into The Betty Ford Center.

The alcoholic entourage, as with the political, goes right along with the delusion. Michiganders are truly a grave lot with a fixation on appearing 'nice'. I think the idiom *"Have a nice day!"* started in some dank corner of the rain-soaked mitten. A well-intentioned mantra. A type of positive affirmation if repeated often enough has the power to alter your reality and if that doesn't do the trick, the cocktail will. Talk about altered reality, it must have been a free-for-all at the Ford Mansion when Betty came out publicly as a pro-choice supporter and an alcoholic. In her defense, it is hard to have a nice day every day in the Great Lake State without some mind-altering drug. I say it was the constant cult-like-politically-charged demand to *"Have a nice day!"* and the total lack of sunshine that finally pushed Betty over the edge. Of course, it wasn't just Betty. Like I said, many of the political wives I met, had a drinking 'issue'. But Betty had the courage and the class to come out and do something positive about the situation. The unhappy wife of Richard Nixon was an alcoholic. She worked the heck out of the martini scene and who could blame her? Watergate was such a muddle and her husband's handle was Tricky Dick, good Lord, she needed a good stiff shot.

It is not just the Republican women who needed to stay half-lit to politic, not by any stretch of the imagination. Just a couple of mentions in the long line of political wives, who had 'issues' with booze; there was Joan Kennedy, whose children had to finally take over as administrators of her affairs because she went from a functional alcoholic to one who simply was too numbed out to manage her life. Kitty Dukakis wrote her book, *"Now You Know'* about her love-hate relationship with alcohol. Kitty was a fall down, pass out drunk, woke up hungover, depending on more booze to stumble through the day. Regardless of the number of times in alcohol treatment, she continued to tip over, drank until she passed flat out, unconscious. Her story, all of their stories could be the story of many a wife of a politician. And, if the rumor mill is at all accurate, true of some of the politician's mistresses to boot.

I believe Betty and Kitty were brave to speak out about their issues with alcohol, to shed light on a very dark subject in political circles. It is why I maintain, w*omen, you must have a strong constitution, to get into politics*. If your man is a politician, you are in politics like it or not, so you better like it! Politics, alcoholics, what is the difference, it's not for the faint of heart. There are far too many drunken politicians and wives of politicians to mention in this guide, mind-bending in fact, goes all the way back to when America was first being developed and water wasn't all that safe to drink.

During my stumping days, I had literally hundreds of small talks with slurring wives of Michigan politicians. We all had the one or two glasses of wine. I remember one in particular in Madonna's hometown. The politico's drunken wife dragged me by the arm into the women's room to 'go off' on some of the constituents who had paid big bucks to attend her husband's fundraiser. She trashed one party member after the next *"Did you get a load of her ridiculous dress, cut down to here?"* She rants as she points to her navel. *"Did you hear what that asshole was saying about Robert?"* Wonder how she goes after the opponents I thought mildly amused. That is when we saw the pair of high heels peeking out from under one of the stalls. She might as well have been 'dishing' into a live microphone Fiorina-style. We bolted before the woman had a chance to flush.

In Ford's hometown one night, a sloshed Justice's wife said to me, *"Don't worry. You will get your mink coat soon enough dear. I got mine after Bill made Supreme Court"*. I had not been concerned about owning a mink and my mistake was not mentioning hers. I smiled and said, *"That's nice."* I had used the phrase *"that's nice"* so many times that year, that I should have had my mouth washed out with soap. I had stolen the punch line from the one joke that I could recite. I am certain you have heard it too, but just in case, here you go girls.

"Two aging southern bells meet for mint juleps at a Kentucky Derby cotillion. Simone says in her sweet southern drawl wagging her ring finger in front of Charlotte's face, *'Darlin' for my 10th wedding anniversary my husband got me this 5 karat diamond* ring.' Charlotte admires Simone's rock saying *'that's nice.'* Simone continues *'and for my 15th anniversary he got me a full-length sable.'* Charlotte's response, *'That's nice!' 'Darlin' this year was your 10th anniversary as I recall. What did your husband get you?'* Simone asks as she sips her mint julep. Charlotte adjusting her bustier replies, *'Why yes darling. He sent me to finishing school. Now, instead of saying 'fuck you I say that's nice'."*

To this day in any social setting when I hear someone say, *"That's nice!"* I stop in my tracks looking for the bitch with the audacity to make such a remark in public. She would be someone I want to meet and maybe hang out with occasionally. Ladies, watch out when a woman replies to you with that tone on her face and says sweetly *'that's nice'.*

THE MOCKTAIL: Faux Mint Julip
1 cup of Apricot juice
1 tsp lime juice
4 fresh mint leaves
Add simple syrup to taste
Alternatively, use confectioners' sugar and a tsp of water to taste.

Muddle three of the mint leaves with the simple syrup
Fill the glass with cracked ice
Stir until the glass gets frosty on the outside
Stemware: Traditional Silver Cup or a Highball Glass
Garnish with fresh mint leaf.

Fortified with my secret one-liner and a not so secret glass of wine I played the political scene stumping for my man. Peter coached me on hiding my wine glass behind my back whenever a camera was nearby. I still have that picture of me at the Governor's mansion, in my white pantsuit, holding a big old glass of wine.

We stumped all over the mitten. Continuously road wary and half-lit we were the 'it-couple' of the hour. At least Peter thought we were and maybe he was right. I don't know. Peter told me often how 'the people' adored us. He said it was our Camelot. While I was getting higher than a kite on the sheer idea of all of that adulation, Peter was insatiable to the point of overdose. Peter needed adoration as a junky needs a fix. He required *all* the attention, *all* the time. Peter was notoriously addicted to the attention of the female persuasion. When I was on top of my game, and truly in character, it did not matter to me. That was just Pete. During the campaign, having to stay on top of my game perpetually bottomed me out. I admit that it tipped me over like a drunk off a bar stool, flat out. At every function, he surveyed the room like a dog on point. With a bead on the most attractive women in the place, he schmoozed with them all before we left. It never occurred to his addled half-in-the-bag mind to use the slightest degree of discretion in his perusal.

One evening, with a glass of wine in my hand, feeling particularly on top of my game, I whispered in his ear: *"Don't you ever get tired of scoping the room for beautiful women?"* I got his politically correct answer: *"No, I always take inventory to ensure that I have the most beautiful one with me,"* he gushed, Irish eyes twinkling giving me his best politician smile. Right on cue, I replied sweetly, *"that's nice."* Yet, compared to Donald, Dewey, Huey, Louie, and a few other ducks in political headlines these days, my guy could be voted man of the year or attain sainthood. OK, perhaps that's taking it a bit too far, exaggerating it a little. That's what I do best!

The campaign trail was an alcohol infused scavenger hunt from the college days. Never knowing what the next stop would bring. We stumped the rubber chicken circuit all over the mitten from Detroit to Mackinaw. It was not the

was that one glass of wine. That is what finally
The campaign consumed my life as theater had,
ad, as my thoughts about life had, as my love
ad. I was heading into Ford's territory again
and right here on the s-curve, the Grand Rapids Press
billboard reminded everybody as if we needed it just what
kind of living hell the winter had been. The gargantuan
billboard displayed a seven-day weather forecast as they
do in the newspaper. Seven mega-sized boxes filled with
gray clouds. In small print below the clouds, it read *so,
what is new?* If it had not been so miserably true, it would
have been funnier. Suffice to say, Michigan winters can be
damn awful harsh. No lie, the official state bird flies south
for the winter. No one has ever spotted the state animal
and I think the state reptile is the lounge lizard.

Running the roads for months on end during the campaign,
I began to see that a change would do me good. OK, a lot
of change would do me good. I tried not to complain. I
tried to mean it when I replied *'you have a nice day
too'*. Nevertheless, somewhere along the way, my
Camelot morphed into an honest to God version of
Camelot. It all fell apart, just like me. Pete and I both got
drunk on what we needed.

THE MOCKTAIL: The Camelot

2 oz. orange juice
2 oz. pineapple juice
1 oz. lemon juice
1/2 oz. simple syrup
1 oz. soda water

Shake up your concoction
Strain into an ice-filled highball glass
Top off with soda water
Garnish with a slice of lemon

The way I figure: If you're going to do a stretch in a place that may not suit you, be married to a person who may not suit you, or intentionally run with a known politician you ought not to trash talk your life blabbing about it all every day. Let us just say I had packed my own dumb lunch and carried a lovely silver corkscrew in my purse.

Your run of the mill part-time lush or co-dependent can become addicted to lots of things far too numerous to list here. There are so many self-help books out there, just grab one off the shelf, sit back and pour yourself a stiff one, light one up because everyone you know could fall into one of the many categories now classified as addictions, including thinking. Just think about that! At any rate, a person who gets into stumping the campaign trail is never going to quit until the race is over and their candidate has won.

Politics can become a dangerous addiction. I do believe there is not one self-help book on the shelf for survivors of a political campaign, winners or losers for that matter. I may have to do something about that. My next story, a self-help book will be entitled, *"Do You Suffer from Post Campaign Stress Syndrome?"* It's either that or one I have been working on for years titled, *"Never Wear a Pantsuit to a Political Function: That's Nice!"* Clearly, that last book has been in the works for some time, as we now see many women in pantsuits at tons of political functions! Yet, for some female politicians that just didn't pay off; you've seen it first hand, but more on that later!

After a year of stumping the Mitten, all the politicians, actors and alcoholics seemed to blend into a blurry sameness at some point along the way. Former President Ford's hometown of Grand Rapids set the stage for the incomparable Charlton Heston, star of the Michigan Judges Association annual celebration. Peter was the President of the Michigan District Judges Association and for that reason alone we were supporting actors that evening. Cocktail hour with Charlton and the ten or fifteen, judiciary leaders was backstage before the show.

Drinking like that without eating, everyone was a bit toasted. Flashing his famous smile, shaking hands and chatting, Charlton was engaging. Peter extraordinarily animated mingled with cohorts. Peter thought I should waltz over, interrupt Charlton and remind him that I played in the cast of that summer stock theater with him, some 18 or 20 years earlier. I declined.   Finally, they called curtain and the dignitaries and their ladies were put into the proper order for entering the room and taking our place on stage. The room was packed with members of the bar as we all entered, announced in royal court fashion, *'the honorable so-and-so'.* Peter, one such so-and-so, had fixed his attention on the 'date' of another judge. He had switched up the procession so that he ended up seated between us, two women. Peter was on my right and the President of the Association of Black Judges of Michigan was to my left. Judge to the left of me, *"joker to the right, here I am, stuck in the middle again!"*

Pete had already had a couple of drinks and had another at his place setting and quickly grew more animated and talkative with the other woman. Pete is just a younger version of your 90-year-old uncle who still hits on twenty-year-old chicks. He is mildly amusing, harmless, obnoxious and somewhat delusional. Those 90-year-old uncles do not just wake up one morning and become a Don Juan it takes years of practice. Their significant other shuffles along beside, thinking the same old thought: *asshole!*

Charlton was hitting full stride, so was Peter. The Judge who brought the other woman was clearly ruffled. These three characters are all drunk I thought. Pretending, that I did not notice the scene, I glanced into the room to see all eyes on the spectacle. Pete put on a show with what's-her-face, for every one of those on-looking barristers, who were also getting snockered. Pete's behavior at this point in the race was reckless. His changing behavior was changing my mind. He even kept the napkin upon which she scribbled: *do you have to work at being an asshole or are you just a natural?* – an abysmal performance and a ridiculous souvenir. She could have asked me. I actually had the correct answer to that question. Yes, it was our Camelot and you know how that story turned out!

Charlton's speech had started out perfectly, stories about how he had played great men, Michelangelo, Julius Cesar, Ben-Hur and even Moses, for God's sake. A towering six-foot-three with chiseled features, Charlton still commanded the stage with his essence and elegance, yet where was this speech going? Was Charlton tanked-up? Did he have an Alzheimer's disorder? Who wrote that speech? Could he not read his cue cards? What was happening? If the whole world is a stage, this whole stage was a world spinning out of control and we the mere bit actors. The judge to my left – let us call him John – started to converse with me. John was artful at talking without moving his lips or actually looking at me directly, the only politically correct way to speak over a world-renowned icon.

Pete could have taken note on how eloquently one can actually chat without moving one's lips or making a scene, to upstage the star on center stage, Charlton. Having done theater did come in handy at times, and yes, we all know *how* to upstage. Yet, one should always refrain! John hoped the evening would end soon. Our little conversation took place without either of us actually looking at the other.

Our mouths barely moved. We were virtual mannequins. Heston never connected the dots between the likenesses of the God-like roles he played to the roles the God-like politician characters played. Too bad, I was writing his lines in my head, I seriously had it mapped out for him. I sat just behind him. I could have passed cue cards to him! That never happened. I just ran his lines for him in my head.

I know the audience got a bigger bang for their buck watching the Pete comedy hour that night. As we were literally fleeing the room, I noticed the miffed Judge, arm around the 'date' escorting her out of reach from Pete. I think he probably accompanied her right out of the building she looked a bit tipsy, ok, a *lot* drunk. John and I barely glanced at one another and I mouthed, *"Good luck!"* He just waved, and rushed off. I would never know how the intriguing story he shared with me ended.

Weeks later still stumping the Mitten, we were guests at Second City in Detroit, Motor City. We were attending a black-tie political soiree and I got my chance. In through the door came John! What a grand entrance he made, all eyes were on him, as they parted to let him pass. John made a deliberate b-line for me!

Great, I thought as he approached; now I can get the lowdown on what happened that night. Eyes still on him as we did the hug and half-kiss thing, taking both my hands he said with an air of familiarity, *"it is so nice to see you, how are you?"* I was so glad to see him too replying, *"Just great. It is wonderful to see you too. I have been dying to hear how it all worked out for you."* He smiled, eyes engaging and asked: *"Remind me, how what turned out?"*

I moved closer and whispered in his ear, *"well, you know, did you go to meet the woman in Oklahoma that night or did you stay home and hope to elude the stalker?"* He dropped my hands he had clung to through my inquiry,

50

regarding me in the most quizzical way as
the very first time in his life saying, *"Y*
confused with someone else." I mumble
I have. Have a nice day!" Both of us
he said as we parted like the Red Sea. I s..,
crowd, tried to blend in and eventually askeu
acquaintance *"Who is that splendid looking black man
over there that I was just kissing?"*

She responded, *"Oh, that is Mayor Archer, I thought you
knew one another!"*

Glancing out of the corner of my eye, lips barely moving,
like a ventriloquist, I said laughingly, *"Yes, me too."*
Decidedly, I wasn't going to tell Peter that story. *"Say,
Peter, how about getting me a glass of wine darling?"*

People think that stars and public figures become drinkers
and drug users because of the spotlight always on them.
But I think alcoholics and drug-users become actors and
politicians.

They need love or need to have a part in life. They are
keen observers of what people want and need. They are
excellent at make believe. They are good at wearing the
mask. They are addicted to a host of things, in particular,
addicted to *winning*. We won!!!

THE MOCKTAIL: Victory Juice

2 oz. orange juice
1/2 oz. lime juice
2 oz. sparkling bitter lemon soda
Add broken ice

Stemware: Wine goblet filled with broken ice

9: Business after Hours: Another Reason to Drink

"It's 4:58 on Friday afternoon. Do you know where your margarita is?" — Amy Neftzger

Business after hours and networkers are the latest iteration of the Seventies three-martini-lunch deal and it has stuck. Somebody got wise to everybody being crocked on the clock and decided that everyone gets hammered after work instead. Plenty of deals are closed when people are just a little drunk. In some cases, one of the parties might be a bit more intoxicated than the other party. Especially after clocking out, alcohol is on the top of the list of most after work functions. In fact, I've heard business associates complain if any after-hours networking event does not serve alcohol as part of the cost of attending. They'll still buy their drinks at the bar, but they're not happy about it.

Entertaining clients is one way companies compete, and after-work socializing is an ever-important and never-ending part of our professional culture. Those who do not participate in the requisite business networking often do not close the deal and may suffer professionally and financially. That's a headache of an entirely different type.

I got the hang of them quickly; get your name badge, head to the bar, and get down to business. When a man is doing business after hours with another man, he can laugh, and talk, and trade business cards and that's just part of doing business. That's the business of doing business and drinking with the boys. Here's a tip: When a woman is doing business after hours with a man and she laughs, talks, and trades business cards, she is the provocateur, in the eye of the shrewd – or perhaps a better word, 'lewd' businessman. It was then, that I realized that I could not have that glass of wine or get at all tipsy because I'd be giving off all the wrong vibes. I learned it's not cool or professional to be slammed at one of those things. Have I been trashed at a few of these events in the past? Oh yes, too many to regurgitate. I said I learned, I did not say how quickly. I got there, though.

How do you work the room at a function? Do you head straight for the bar to get your cocktail and hang around up there? You might want to rethink that a bit. Typically, I find a place and sort of hold court. If the court isn't busy, I may change locations until I locate the center and am then able to converse with a variety of people as one-on-one conversation is not necessarily my forte. I am much better in a larger group. I often hold a Champaign flute, the same one all night long and don't drink any of it.

Here is how that worked out for me recently at a cool gig at the Sunset Marquis: At the Morrison Gallery West Hollywood event called *Cars & Stars*, I met Billy Gibbons, guitar man and lead singer of ZZ Top, and that was a treat. I hung on to my champagne flute until I grew tired of it and planted it in a planter. A reporter was watching me plant that flute, placing it in just the right way, an artist at work; I looked at him and said: *"I call it champagne in the planter."* I smiled, and he smiled. I said, *"it looks lovely there don't you agree?"* He only said, *"I do."* Billy was super chill, with that famous beard and wearing those sunglasses all night. Hell, when you are that cool, the sun shines all the time. Fans were clamoring for the photos with him and getting their books signed. I waited until the fan fest was just about over, walked up, and said: *"I would just like to shake the hand of a legend."* He smiled and shook my hand. A few photographers I knew, started yelling, Zoe over here over here, I felt like a celebrity for half-a-second, but it was all about the man of the hour. Billy smiled at me asking, *"should we look like we are just hanging out?"* I replied, *"Well yeah that's a plan."* That made him smile and chuckle a bit and we cozied up. My friend, the famous Rock N' Roll photographer, Jimmy Steinfeldt, was there of course and got a cool shot of that interaction. It's a special keepsake – e*specially, since the only time in my entire life I got stopped for speeding, it was all Billy Gibbon's fault. That's right, Billy was essentially the Star in my Car story!*

Author Zoe Robinette takes things over the ZZ Top, first with Billy Gibbons at a Hollywood party – then while pulled over for speeding – blaming 'Legs' for her rockin' the gas pedal.

So, here's my story: I've always loved ZZ Top and one very-very early morning I was listening to *Sharp Dressed Man, Legs, Gimme All Your Lovin'* and the rest of the best grooves with speakers turned up full volume, while I had my pedal to the metal.

I was driving nearly 90-miles-an-hour down a long deserted road, I felt like I was flying. ZZ had given me some wings that morning. There were no cars for miles and miles and I had a long way to go and a short time to get there. The road was empty, except for that one cop, who came out of nowhere. When he finally got my attention and pulled me over he announced, *"Do you realize I had to do nearly 100 miles an hour to catch you?"*

I was stunned and demanded in total shock, *"Why would you do that?"* He just took off his hat and scratched his head, *"to catch up to you; miss, have you have any idea how fast you were driving?"*

Still shocked, I replied, *"No, I am fairly certain it was close to the speed limit though"* looking around for a speed limit sign.

He disagreed, saying that I was over the speed limit by about 40 miles per hour and inquired emphatically *"What were you thinking?"* I could have answered, *"My Head's in Mississippi"* just for kicks, but refrained (he didn't look all that happy with me at the moment). He leaned into my automobile to smell for signs of alcohol. It had been more than five hours since I had a cocktail, and only one, just one I tell you because I was driving. Thankfully, I didn't have to blow into the tube.

I told him I had ZZ Top blaring and that southern fried rock and roll just put me in a grove, with my foot a little heavy on the metal, I guess. I turned up the tune a little for him to hear and he couldn't help but laugh. *"Listen,*

*you gave me a run today, but I do not want to catch you
out here driving like this again or I will throw the book at
you. Do you understand?"* Yes officer, thank you.

And, thank you, Billy and ZZ Top for giving me good
times, great driving and dancing music and some very
sweet memories. Had I been drinking and cruising 40
miles over the limit, I would have had a big bad case of
the *"Certified Blues"* baby!

THE MOCKTAIL: The Chaser

1/4 oz. passion-fruit syrup
2 oz. pineapple juice
1/2 oz. lime juice
1 slice pineapple

Throw plenty of crushed ice in the blender
Strain and fill with more crushed ice
Garnish with a slice of pineapple and chase it with another
one!
Stemware: Highball Glass

Actually, my lesson began years earlier at a business after-
hours function that inspired me to handle them with more
grace, than I had previously; while seated at the table of an
Episcopalian Fund Raiser, in San Francisco, with John
Day, Denise Brown, and Martin Sheen. I am perfectly
aware that name-dropping is not chic. Yet, the point is,
when we look to those with celebrity status, we imagine
that their lives are beautiful beyond imagination. Well,
probably most of the time they are! Their real stories about
issues we all face tend to level the playing field, in a
manner we relate to.

Martin did not make light of his sobriety or his drunken
past, although, he was witty of course. It was his

authenticity, his grace and unmistakable charm that shone through, as he shared his story. He made us laugh, and caused us to reflect.

I admired Martin's courage, conviction, and candor. He is quite a man. He told us that getting sober, literally saved his life. It took him awhile to get there but he did and that matters in the course of one's life. In a word, he exemplified an unmistakable class. As we were leaving, he said, *"I will see you later Zoe."*

I just smiled, knowing I'd most likely never lay eyes on him again, in real life. Real life is such a funny expression. I have often said that I have had *near life experiences* while others profess to have near death experiences. It's all in one's perspective, real life.

Denise was there to talk with us about building safe homes for abused and battered women. Her story was compelling and yes, there are often severe episodes of drinking involved around the issue of battered women.

Absolutely everyone has a story to tell, everyone has been there, no matter his or her station in life.

Finding your truth, finding your passion and getting happy, is as close as one can come to living the good life and having it all!

THE MOCKTAIL: The Schmooze

You can schmooze all you like without the booze!
12 oz. orange juice
12 oz. 7-Up® soda

Cracked ice
Add Orange Juice and 7-up®
Stir, and then add ice.
Stemware: Champagne Flute

10: What's a Nice Girl like Me Doing Getting
Kicked Out of a Dump like This?

"There comes a time in every woman's life when the only thing that helps is a glass of champagne."
— **Bette Davis**

I've been kicked out of a few places back in the younger days; check! Not all by myself, I had friends who helped make that happen. I am definitely not proud of the bounce factor but welcome to the dark side.

Did you know that drunken women talk louder? It's true that drinking makes you talk louder than normal. It is as if your own ears get drunk and cannot hear a single word you are slurring, creating the hideous loud high-pitched drunk speak. You've all have heard it; you know exactly what I mean. The loudness factor alone will get you kicked out of a fine establishment. Did you know that drunken loud singing in unison with your friends could also get you bounced? *"Drums keep pounding a rhythm to the brain- La de da de de, la de da de da."* [The Beat Goes on – Sonny Bono]

Did you know that drunken women don't dance half as well as they think they do? Did you know dancing until you tip over with your blitzed-out boy toy (doing his best to impress with his suave moves and that long deep dip) can also get you kicked out of a joint? Actually, you have to be "dipped and tipped" a few times before they label you a safety hazard to yourself and others and have you removed from the dance floor, and the establishment. However, they let you leave with your keys. Yes, they do.

58

I find that crazy, so does Brittney, Paris, Lindsey Lohan and so many others, too numerous to mention. The only reason *they* got the DUI instead of half of you reading this guide, was that the paparazzi hovers, and so do the police: They don't let the glamorous stars out of their sight.

I let a casual acquaintance talk me into a 40-something birthday celebration. Actually, one of the biggest little party girls in San Francisco was hosting this party.

She was a little tiny gal that had every feature on her body enhanced or enlarged. She was especially proud of her chichis and well she should be: They were a pretty big deal.

 She was a darling girl, but all the enhancements somehow aged her, as in adding years to what may have been a youngish attractive girl.

Sometimes her lips would get lumpy looking or one of her cheeks was fuller and I knew she needed to go in, for whatever they were pumping into her little 40-year-old body.

The problem for this little Southern belle was, she never ate, and she drank much more than the teaspoon of the alcohol, it took to intoxicate her. It was as if she did not know she could maintain her buzz and stop drinking booze.

Once buzzed, she kept on drinking. Once in a state of inebriation, all inhibitions if she had any, to begin with, went right out the window.

She and I had both dated one of the physicians on staff and I think he was all we actually had in common. Naturally, he attended my birthday party. She meant well.

The festivities – or shall we call them fiascos – started at the W in San Francisco, where we all gathered for before-dinner cocktails.

The cast that evening was a mix of business and social, so it was going to be interesting to navigate with the grace it required. I decided my best bet was to *Mocktail* the entire evening. I arranged it with the bartender to be sure to make my faux Cosmopolitan, served, glamorously, in the sexy martini glass that I loved to hold onto at an event.

When someone offered to buy me another birthday celebratory drink, I would say, *"Oh I don't know if I should, but why not, it's my birthday. I like my Cosmo made a very particular way. Please tell the bartender that this one is for the birthday girl, and to make it exactly like the last one he knows how I like them. Thanks, sweetie."*

I was chatting with someone, while the little southern belle was bending over and shoving her cleavage into some man's face that had the audacity to ignore her. Big chi-chis in his face suddenly got his attention.

This was going on while someone else decided to duck-tape one of the sexy women in our soiree to a pillar because she was a bad little girl. Turns out the doctor had dated her too. What can I say? The doctor was in the house – all over town!

The wait staff was doing their best to control the scene, but it was apparently getting out of hand. It was when we started to leave on our own accord that the bouncers bounced us all out of there.

But as I was making my way across the expansive floor without so much as one ounce of alcohol in my body, my bevy of hot girls decided to do a little hoochie-dance around me and it caused quite a spectacle, as they intended.

Being in the center, I could not just stand there as a ditz could I? That would look bad. I just twirled and dipped, bumped and "grinded" a little, ok maybe expertly, pretty much did the girl in the middle bit.

I knew we should be getting out of the main lobby with this little number, but the bouncers just played ring around the rosy with us and escorted us outside. Something along the lines of a cattle round-up.

This ticked off the little hostess, who yelled at the bouncer in her darling southern drawl, *"Hey you, I've been kicked out of better places than this!"* and happy birthday to me.

Thankfully, I was 100% cocktail free, had a Mock Cosmo in my hand all night long.

Everyone imagined I was as tanked as the rest, as I downed quite a few faux Cosmos!

Yet darlings, I was thoroughly amused watching the show and it was quite a show.

I have so many memories of that night. Having those memories just reaffirmed my distaste in having birthday parties that centered on me in any way.

Leave it to Oscar Wild to sum it up with all the wit it actually takes *"Alcohol, taken in sufficient quantities, may produce all the effects of drunkenness."*

THE MOCKTAIL: The Juicy Princess
1 oz. Grenadine syrup
2 oz. Grape juice
1 oz. Apple juice
1 tbsp. Vanilla syrup
1 tbsp. Lemon juice
Stir over ice
Garnish with a lime slice
Stemware: Highball Glass

11: Parlez-vous Français?

"I only drink Champagne on two occasions: When I am in love and when I am not."
- Coco Chanel

I absolutely adore the French and am proud of that half of my family tree. However, I totally hate having birthday parties. I always have and always will. After reaching age, 40 there should be a mandated cut off on birthday celebrating. It is seriously depressing.

No woman looks forward to turning fifty freaking years old. In my case, I had it planned to be pushing up daisies by that time. I mean, fifty is ancient and I certainly had celebrated enough to cut some years off my life. However, I had to live with it, just like everyone else! To do that I had to get my mind wrapped around the fact that I had lived a half-century on planet Earth. Where I lived before that, I am not quite certain.

I surely was not going to let any of my so-called friends throw me one of those over the hill parties, as they did when I turned forty. This group of do-gooders had a 15-wheeler bring a big neon flashing sign to my house and plant it in my front yard while I was teaching night school at the University. It may have been a regular truck, but I imagined a 15-wheeler all the same.

I still have the incriminating photos of my son on the front lawn conspiring with the vandals, otherwise known as my friends, who put those '40s' all over that sign. For years after, people would say, *"oh yeah I know where you live, I saw that sign in your yard that year."* Well, sure they did, you could see that blasting blinking sign for miles. I did have a few drinks nightly to get over the trauma of seeing it there, every day for the entire week. I felt like moving. Oh, that's right, I did move.

Turning fifty is an ugly word that starts with F and is utterly horrifying. I went alone to France, just to be adored by young French men, for my fiftieth birthday month and to avoid any sort of over the hill party. Being alone allows one to let life-altering experiences sink in and lets one grieve a significant loss [youth in this case] in peace.

I loved everything about celebrating what would be the first half-century of life in a place of my heritage. What's not to love about France and the French people? I mean really, it's the only way to sashay over the hill ladies. Trip Tip: Stay at least a month: It takes that long to let major life events sink in gracefully. Find your apartment, settle in and celebrate being you!

Each morning at the same time, I went to my favorite boulangerie and the same handsome waiter would seat me and get me my usual. In the afternoon, I would hit the *plage*, the beachfront at Le Negresco and sunbathe. The Cannes Film Festival was going on, and there would often be photographers getting shots of their stars on the plage.

One afternoon while getting my sun a woman next to me, most likely my age asked in French if I would like to try her spray mist. Yes, of course, I would! I had not seen this particular item before and she had several mist bottles so we sat and took our sun and spritzed ourselves regularly. Finally, as the sun was setting we parted and she left me with one of the bottles.

I went to the market immediately after to find the same mist bottle to blend in and be conspicuously French. There it was, I got a couple of those bottles, and to my surprise, they were not as expensive as I imagined they might be; my new friend was quite chic. Upon closer inspection, I discovered that I was spraying water all over myself all day and literally frying myself to a crisp. I was not worried, though, *c'est la vie.*

Early each evening I went back to the town square to the little café to order a glass of red wine. Everyday about the same time there were two older gentlemen there having their wine and conversing. I loved the casual pace in Vieux Nice. It had a calming effect on me. No one grabbed a latte to go slurping it down like a heathen in a fat-ass rush to get some place. I adored these people. One afternoon one of the older men asked in French if I was a gymnast or dancer and I responded yes to both. That got quite a conversation going, but I was at a loss within five minutes, with the sheer cadence and level of French.

The next afternoon they saw me again and motioned for me to join them. The smaller of the two men had a scrapbook with him. He had been an Olympic gymnast medalist for France in his younger days. He had his pictures with him getting his medals. He then settled in Nice, to train young female Olympic gymnast hopefuls. I was all smiles and naturally gushed over his scrapbook, as becoming an Olympian is truly a feat that many can only dream of, one that he had mastered.

His associate a larger buff man was a wrestler defected from Russia who also trained Olympians. The following afternoon, the two gentlemen motioned me over again, and I did my best to speak French, as neither of the men spoke a bit of English.

On this afternoon, a blonde woman rode up to the café on her bicycle. I will never forget her grand arrival. She was beautiful, dressed in black slacks, Hepburn style, and the most awesome leopard skin high heels. They introduced her to me as Billy. She spoke fabulous English having lived in New York for some time. She told me in English that the men, her old friends had invited her to join us so that our conversation actually made sense. She whispered the gymnast wanted a date with me and we laughed.

Billy did not drink wine as the three of us were drinking. She took me into her confidence and told me that Parisian women did not drink wine, they drank only champagne. Certainly, drinking wine in public was not chic. Ladies in France did not drink that horrible wine. However, I had been seen drinking that awful wine every day for a couple of weeks, Oh Mon Dieu the shame of it.

I know I must have turned the very shade of my red wine and laughed. Billy and I became instant friends and went to the Opera, the Symphony and to Monte Carlo, Monaco where she had very close friends. She took me everywhere and showed me the way very unique natives, lived. She was a principal real estate agent for the principality.

When Billy and I took a stroll up the steps in Monaco or on other lesser inclines, she would often have to stop and sit to catch her breath. She was so frail. Then I realized I had never seen Billy eat a bite of food in all the time we spent together. Surely she ate, but what and when I do not know. She lived mainly on espresso as far as I could tell. She also said that French ladies do not have any kind of dairy product added to their afternoon coffee. She taught me so much! She was my new idol.

My days in the sun had come to an end and it was time to say adieu to my France, and I cried. I went to my usual café to say good-bye to my sweet gay waiter boy; he had gotten into the most darling habit of flagging me past the waiting crowds to seat me at my regular table. This morning was no different aside from it was my last visit to his café. He brought my espresso to the table nearly in tears, as they had no chocolate croissants that morning. I pouted a little and the next thing I knew, he was running across the square to another café and brought me a fresh baked chocolate croissant. So sweet, it made me want to cry. I love the French. We hugged again at our last farewell.

The gymnast had invited Billy and me to attend one of his girl's gymnastic meets, and I was delighted to play the role of the American gymnastic judge on that delightful spring day. I realized that one could do what they loved and have the world all tied up in a cute little bow no matter how old they got. I would miss him, the wrestler, and the waiter at our café on the square. I showed up to say my final good-byes and the waiter gave me an autographed postcard of the café where I had met my new friends.

The birthday celebrating my half-century on planet earth changed my life in many profound ways. I had this beautiful collection of people from every lifestyle to thank for my new attitude. The older gentlemen showed me that they could still do what they loved despite their age. In particular, I had Billy to thank for showing me the finer side of the South of France; the way natives live and I appreciated her company. They all had the most direct effect on my mind and my future.

They taught me a lot. Yet, I learned the hard way, that you cannot get a taxi to stop when you are carrying more than one large-size purse in France. Seriously, have skis, oh too bad they drive on by. Have a purse and two bags, sorry they wave as they pass you by. Try hiding the bags and when they stop, grab them quickly, as they drive off with the door hanging open leaving you on the street. This little cabbie factoid plays a significant role in my final day or two in France.

My sojourn was ending and I was on a mission to buy some fabulous French wines. I had a list of these handpicked great wines, from a friend who ran a restaurant in San Francisco. He recommended I bring some back, and even gave me a few hundred to buy some for the café. Therefore, I did that near the end of the trip.

What was I thinking? Oh yes, I was thinking wine, lots of wine. I had my shopping cart full of bottles of French wine and upon check out discovered the store did not ship. Would that put an end to my wine-mad hatter-shopping spree? Really, are you kidding? No, I was not to be defeated! I decided I would find another place and get it shipped. I dragged the overflowing cart of wine out in front of the upscale shop where I had purchased it and tried in vain to hail a cab. No way would a French cabbie stop to help a woman with a shopping cart full of wine. The beautiful place I was staying at was only a few long blocks away.

In Vieux Nice, cars cannot actually get down the narrow cobblestone streets, so I pushed my cart of wine all the way to my apartment. I felt like a wine street vendor shuffling along, but no one knew me. They did not know me, but they sure heard me coming for blocks. They may have possibly seen me here or there, during my month or so stay, but technically, just a few people there actually knew me.

The door attendant looked at me as if I was truly insane, as I without a single ounce of hesitation, pushed my shopping cart full of wine into the luxe lobby. He had everything he could do to keep from laughing, as I squeezed my body in, next to the cart on the lift, to get my stash to my second-floor room. A spectacle never to be repeated there, I am certain, and may well be a story told there too, by now. If you have heard that story, yep, that was I!

Well, what is a girl to do with all this wine? I took myself to a nearby wine store and asked the woman if she would ship it to me. She smiled warmly saying in her fabulous

French accent, *"Oh my no. No one will ship wine from Nice my dear, no one does, as someone might steal it."* I told her I was confident that no one would mess with the box in San Francisco. It would be all right. She laughed at me in the lovely singsong way French women do, *"Oh no, I do not mean Americans will steal it. It won't make it out of town, our Frenchmen will take it!"*

She was still laughing, as I walked back out to the cobblestone street, to get a drink and figure out a plan for my bootleg. I thought about that commercial where the gorilla works for an airline and throws every piece of luggage he handles, he kicks it, stomps on it and voila, the luggage is so fabulous, no matter how hard the gorilla tries, it holds up. Well, the plan did not have anything to do with that commercial. The plan was to go purchase one of those gigantic, soft-sided bags, from the tourist section of town. They are so huge that a small pony could actually live in one of those things. I got my big cheap bag, wrapped each bottle in a plastic bag and then wrapped it again, inside my garments. I could barely slog it to the lift and drag it down a few more cobblestone blocks to the train station. I was dragging, and the wheels on the big old cheap bag were dodgy, doing their best to stay intact.

Hoisting the bag on and off the train, such delight, the day I left for the aêroport, there was just one last spectacle. I had to jostle it on to the train with a full body press. Leave them laughing is my motto!

Why I hadn't called on the wrestler for help is beyond me! I just smirked, thinking, yes I bought a lot of cool stuff while I was here, just another bourgeois American.

In line at customs, when asked if I had anything to declare, I realized there was nothing at all to report, announce, disclose aside from telling the nice man with the badge, that I was just sad to be leaving, nearly in tears in fact. The man was empathic, of course, I was sad to be leaving his glorious France. He stamped my passport and took the bag. It was so heavy that a gorilla juicing, pumped up on steroids could not have lifted that thing.

I paid a tariff for the weight, not much, a lot less than shipping would have been. If the gorilla cannot lift the bag, he cannot throw the bag, so voila, the precious cargo was safe.

Back at SFO, I recognized that huge bag immediately, with the big red **HEAVY** warning labels plastered on the sides, so no unsuspecting baggage handler would end up with a hernia, trying to lift that thing.

Every bottle made it home unbroken.

My fiftieth birthday, celebrating half-a-century on planet earth, my way, was the most fabulous birthday of my life. I felt reborn. I was ready to live my real life! *Vive la France!*

MOCKTAIL: Bogus Bubbly

1-ounce sparkling white grape juice
1-ounce ginger ale
1-ounce apple juice
3 fresh raspberries, for garnish (it isn't always easy to get fresh raspberries so strawberries work too)
Stemware:
5-ounce fabulous champagne flute
In a champagne flute, combine ginger ale, grape, and apple juice. (Do not add ice.) Garnish with raspberries.

12: Change Will Do You Good

"Nothing lasts forever. So live it up, drink it down, laugh it off, avoid the drama, take chances and never have regrets because at one point everything you did was exactly what you wanted" - Marilyn Monroe

Change often does one good, but not the change of life. The change of life is such a dead end street to travel, no exit except for ashes blowing in the wind, while your kids read the fun adventurous stories about your life, from the cue cards you wrote for them. When you are in your twenties and even into your forties, you think you are somehow magically immune to this state of being. *This state of being is otherwise known as, the state of shock.*

Trust me, if you live long enough you will change. No matter who you are, drinking alcohol during and after the infamous hideous change of life is an absolute nightmare.

The only place a woman in the change or post-change should drink alcohol, is home alone, with her partner, husband, or best friend, who could care less, if she suddenly has the fattest tongue on the planet.

If I drink a bit of wine and hear my voice sound as if I was stinking drunk, while my head says, *"no way, I am seriously not inebriated."* I've labeled this, phenomena *"Fat Tongue Syndrome."* This rare syndrome I have discovered hasn't reached medical circles, yet.

If she does not have to say anything, a woman can only smile and nod in agreement at the appropriate times; is in the safety of her own home, so she does not have to maneuver around any strange furniture arrangements, or if served adequate amounts of food, she can have a drink.

Otherwise, she's one of the *"Absolutely Fabulous"* characters, darling. How I related to those two women – they could be any of us, best show ever! She could wind up being the mom on *"Arrested Development"* or Charlie Sheen's mother, on *"Two-and-a-Half Men"*. I found every one of those women extremely humorous. I would not mind being any of them actually, but after I retire…

Back to reality, this is real life and it is tough to try and have even a half glass of wine at a cocktail party, business after hours networking event, a political event, and lately, at most wedding receptions, they serve lots of alcohol and not much food. However, if she has eaten sufficiently, she can have some libations, mixed in with her Mocktails. A woman who has completely changed must change her alcohol drinking habits as well. You know who you are. Simply add some spicy Mocktails into the mix at any and all of these events.

Overall, the change of life in America is much harder than it is for women in Europe, from my perspective. Younger men actually adore older women in Europe, at least in France, as I recall.

However, thanks to Madonna, Tina, Demi and plenty of others, the older woman younger man thing is also changing; it is becoming an American thing. Yet, in America, they call us women of a certain age, *Cougars*, who have liaisons with younger men. That is not at all an attractive depiction of the sophisticated lady. That label needs to *change* and that will do us all good. What do we call an older man dating a younger woman? Oh yes, we call him a man.

Still, America is addicted to youth; severely addicted to being youthful.

I often remark that I am terribly immature. However, that has nothing at all to do with youth, apparently.

Americans are so addicted to appearing young that there seems to be no end in sight. Injections, peels, lasers, Botox©, fillers, *Lifestyle Lift©*, mid-face lift, full face lift, ponytail lift©, cheek implants, chin implants, brand new manufactured perfect teeth, breast enlargement, and ass enlargement. Let's pause here just a second. Is it just me, or does Kim Kardashian's derriere have a life of its own? I mean, seriously.

Kim's posterior holding up a martini glass: There it is, advertising heaven: both alcohol *and* the big bootie. The ass enlargement craze is the one enlargement, I would love to discuss with women who have had the procedure.

I do not know and cannot even speculate, as to whether Kim has had ass implants. I do know that buttock implants are quite popular these days, with girls in an attempt to have the famous Kim keister. I have tried to sit on tennis balls or bags of frozen peas before and it is truly difficult. I want to know if it feels like you might tip sideways or if your butt ever aches. That would give an entirely new meaning to the age old saying *"what a pain in the ass!"*

THE MOCKTAIL: Passion Bootie
1/4 oz. passion-fruit syrup
2 oz. pineapple juice
1/2 oz. lime juice
1 slice pineapple
Blend with crushed ice.
Strain; fill with crushed ice

Stemware: Highball Glass

I do *think* about getting my ass back in *shape* every day. Thinking about it does not move me to action. Yet, I get up every morning and say I should work out today. I have said that to myself every day for some time. I just needed a little inspiration if I was going to get those gams and glutes back into condition. I think I may have found that inspiration recently, having attended the Joan Collins exhibit, at the famous Julien's in Los Angeles.

Yes, I will name drop again because most of you know exactly whom I'm talking about. If you're not sure, do yourself a favor and look Joan up. Joan looked fabulous, darling, and I mean incredible! Her legs and her body were tight. She is 83 years old ladies, yet women in their 30s should have such a fine body and toned legs, she is a shining example of keeping that mojo going.

For any of you, perusing *Party like a Mock Star!,* who've never seen Joan Collins, you must look her up. In her younger days – the age you may be right now – she was a glamorous bombshell. Moreover, compare her 83-year-old rocking body to the one you are living in now, and thank me for sharing this story with you. You may need a bit of inspiration yourself. You can thank me later.

Yes, I think seeing Joan up close and personal gave me the inspiration to begin to jump in and get my mojo going again.

There, at the event, I found myself in the presence of the beautiful Jacqueline Bisset, one of my favorite movie icons, and we took in all of Joan's fabulous garments from the *"Dynasty"* era of her life. Joan was just as flamboyant as ever, her entrance, the entrance only a true star can make, was spectacular. She is simply, a siren, even at her age. We should all aspire to be as in shape as Joan.

Jacqueline is relaxed and comfortable in her own skin; she is the essence of class. She was gracious and looked stunning, just gorgeous for a woman who is 70 years old.

She is naturally radiant and being photographed beside the beautiful Jacqueline was so much fun! I absolutely loved the photo taken that evening of Jacqueline and I (below), by well-known photographer, Ivor Levine.

Author Zoe Robinette hanging out with Jacqueline Bisset

I thought Jacqueline was most beautiful in, *Dangerous Beauty,* a movie made from an actual story of Venetian Courtesans. Jacqueline played the part of the older woman. The age I refer to in this bit about, *"Change Will do You Good."*

In the movie, Jacqueline was training the younger beauty in the art of becoming the perfect companion to the Royals, to the kings. The younger woman carefully shaped in the gorgeous image of Jacqueline, who had the charm, wit, and beauty, without the lineage to marry one of those good fellows. Courtesans were educated in every manner of cavorting with royalty. I felt Jacqueline brought such grace and charm to that role, simply a woman with class.

Party Like a Mock Star

More to the point, I remember the press blasting her on her acceptance speech at the Golden Globes, for her award-winning role, she played in "*Dancing on the Edge*." Again, watch that one, and please skip the Golden Globes presentation. The idiotic press accused her of being drunk.

According to my sources, they just threw her onstage, without a meal served beforehand, out of the pre-determined scheduled lineup. Look at how that worked out, she was literally '*Dancing on the Edge*' during that acceptance speech. Oh my, she used the word 'shit' on stage, which one among of us has not used that word. They threw her a wild curve ball and expected 70-year-old Jacqueline to maintain her legendary class.

Yet, Jacqueline's only misstep was not at all her fault. I suspect although I do not know for certain, and I am not saying this as fact, that she may have had a sip of champagne, just before they threw her on stage. Maybe she hadn't had a sip at all, for all I know. Just the fact that they gave her no warning and pushed her on stage that way, would be enough to make anyone *dance on the edge*. Mocktail or Cocktail, speech as it may be, Jacqueline is always a class act.

THE MOCKTAIL: Dangerous Beauty Pink Champagne

1/2 cup sugar
1 1/2 cups water
1/2 cup orange juice
2 cups cranberry juice
1 cup pineapple juice
2 bottles sparkling ginger ale
Boil sugar and water until the sugar dissolves, and allow cooling. Stir cranberry, pineapple, and orange juice, and chill. Just before you serve, add the carbonated beverage to give it the bubbles. *Don't add the carbonated beverage too soon – stick to the plan!*

13: The Buzz on Dating and Mating

"May you - Work like you don't need the money, love like you've never been hurt, dance like no-one is watching, screw like it's being filmed, and drink like a true Irishman" – a true Irishman

Why do non-alcoholic men seem so damn boring? Is it just me? No, I am confident that it is *not* just me. I do not like to ring my own bell, but I admit that I am a very gifted woman. I possess one of the most finely honed, yet very natural talents for choosing high profile successful men, who are also high-level functioning drunks.

Conversely, those same men choose me when I am not even looking. Actually, I can attract and be attracted to an alcoholic in any setting, alcohol not included. I am not crying in my beer over this fact, nor am I out celebrating this fact. It is just a fact. I can pick them out of a line-up!

My radar for selecting alcoholics is so exceptional that not so long ago I fell in love at first sight with a photo of a man on an Internet dating site. That is correct; you read that correctly I fell in love with a picture.

I am not in my twenties, thirties, or forties anymore but honestly, this man's face had an intoxicating effect on me. Seriously, I had it all together at the time. I had done the work on myself, for years; even read *'Calling in the One'* had done most, if not all of the exercises in the book. I was ready to call in *"The One."* Much like a duck hunter uses the duck mating call gizmo to lure in the poor soon to be a "dead duck," I imagine.

For those of you who have never joined the Internet dating scene, I will give you my version of the entire virtual meat market right now. They send you literally hundreds and hundreds of photos of men to choose from, every week. Imagine that, you do not even have to put on make-up to shop for a man. Men being men, they jump right in and try to seduce you into the date of your life. Right out of the gate, they want a date. The sheer number of invites requires one to either hire a social secretary to screen them or quit your job and make dating a full-time occupation.

Those of you, who have tried the internet dating site, know exactly what I mean. I am sure you will agree, that you feel like the homecoming Queen, cheerleader, the hard bodied Frosh on campus during the rush-week again and get a kick out of all those emails, likes, winks, and other equally juvenile ways of virtual flirting, to find *The One*.

I read the letters of introduction or the *"you look like fun want to hang out?"* messages and turned down most of them. That is not entirely accurate. I turned down everyone and hid my profile for the first three months. I was not emotionally equipped to handle online dating for heaven's sake! I am sensitive and it was overwhelming.

I continued to hang out with my girlfriends and my gay, pretty-boy friends, all of whom love to dress up, dance and laugh a lot. Requisites in friendship are dressing up from time to time, dancing, and laughing, heavy on the laughing!

Back to dating and mating: I had not been in love for years, oh so many years. The real big deal was I had not had sex in about six years. *I was a born again virgin.* So, after listening to all my girlfriends tell me to get back in there and have fun. I gave Internet dating another whirl. Again, a rush hour traffic hoard of men, but I was savvier this time. I realized I did not have to reply politely to anyone. I could simply ignore everything and everyone who was simply unappealing one way or another. That cut down on the need to hire secretarial assistance. Then one day, a face looked directly into my face online of course. I knew instantly, this man was the one man I had to have. I cannot tell you why it had to be him, but, it had to be him. I 'liked' his photo. That was the extent of my engagement. He wrote back immediately, thanking me gave me his name and asked for mine. He made me a *'favorite'* right away. I opened up my dating.com site like a crack addict to look at his face every day. I just needed that fix.

We dated.

The first date, we were quite engaged with our story and each other. We closed down the place, never realizing that all the tables and chairs from the outside patio were taken in, and the wait staff had all disappeared.

Very quietly, as if he hated to disturb us, the owner of the café, told us his establishment had closed several hours before.

The One told the owner we would be back. In the parking lot, he walked me to my car and kissed me so passionately, that I thought my knees would buckle. He asked quietly, *"did I hear you say you loved me?"*

I heard the question. I backed up a bit, to take him in and did not respond. I swear at that moment, I could have said yes to just about anything. Let us not forget, I was a born again virgin.

He tucked me into my car and gave me another little kiss. He had some miles to drive and I a few short blocks.

When I got home, he texted, *"I think we are on to the start to something amazing."* I agreed, and lay there for some time, contemplating this man.

Smiling, I feel asleep. Over time, and unbeknownst to this poor duck aka *The One*, he recited every line I had written to myself, through my yet unknown lover's eyes.

THE MOCKTAIL: The Mindbender

1 oz. orange juice

1/2 oz. lemon juice

1 tsp grenadine syrup

5 oz. ginger ale

[handwritten annotations: "1/8 cup", "1 Table spoon", "X 2 makes only one drink"]

Fill your Mocktail shaker half-full with ice first.

Pour the orange juice, lemon juice, and grenadine into your exquisite Mocktail shaker, and shake it up baby! Top it with it off with ginger ale, stir well. Be prepared to have your mind bent.

Stemware: Highball Glass

"Calling in The One" is really an excellent book. Written by Katherine Thomas, she has you write yourself a letter as if you were your lover. You tell yourself all the things your true love would say. You mail the letter to yourself and wait for the universe to send you *'The One.'* What's-his-name was my true love, *The One;* I'd been waiting for, forever. This man was a freaking love song in my heart. We continued to close down restaurants, night after night.

I asked him once; if he recalled the question, he asked me in the parking lot on our first rendezvous. "No" was his reply. He did not ask me what it was or why I asked, we let it float off into the nether land. Retrospectively, I recognize, that was a recurring theme. Letting things float off into outer space. When people asked how we met, I said *"you know the traditional way, on-line"* or we made up ridiculous stories for people to amuse ourselves. His acquaintances would comment in our presence, on how truly beautiful and uplifting it was to see two people so obviously in love. They would take me aside to tell me I was the best-suited woman they had ever seen the man with, adding, they had seen him with many. We made people happy about love and that fueled the delusion – that and copious amounts of the finest wines, a few pills, and a little weed. Looking back, I have to smile; he was an amusing stand-up lay down alcoholic. When people asked how we broke up, I told them *"He dumped me, you know, the traditional way, through an email."*

THE MOCKTAIL: Faux Fruity Passion
4 oz. passion-fruit syrup
A dash cranberry juice
A dash lemon juice
10 - 12 oz. club soda
Mix simple syrup and juices to your glass top with chilled club soda.
Garnish with a cherry
Stemware: Collins Glass

My gift of falling for an alcoholic is so grand and deeply ingrained. I have to take you back to my younger years to get this story right. It was college days 1972. I fell in love at first sight with the picture of a lead guitar player of a Latin rock band. Yes, I have actually fallen in love at first sight with two photographs. I also fell in love with a voice on the phone once, but I digress.

So, there was this young, hot, Latino. Do they make them any other way? He was the lead guitarist for a sizzling Latin rock band. They had a sexy #1 hit that I repeatedly played, just to hear my man, on his sweet guitar. He was playing to me. *No, Chicca, he was playing me.* I put the picture of him on my wall, in my dorm, and swooned over him daily.

I told my friends, *"I know he would love me if we ever met"* convinced we were star-crossed lovers. Of course, life went on with a series of alcoholic deadheads to fall for to keep me spinning for a few decades. Fast forward to the dazzling summer of 1999, La Raza Park in San Francisco listening to an awesome Latin rock band, I danced in the sun enjoying the heck out of myself. Just as I was leaving, a tall, dark, handsome Latino made his way up the hill to talk with me. He had on a Hawaiian type shirt and wore dark sunglasses, jeans, and red converse tennis shoes.

The presence of his body close to mine, made my heart sing, and my kundalini spirits dance. I felt woozy, and no, I was not drinking! I melted at the sound of his velvety soft smooth voice. I was madly in love at first sight. *"I am sorry I didn't get your name,"* I said. He apologized, as he introduced himself, and took off his sunglasses, so I could fall hopelessly, into his warm brown eyes. I was slightly embarrassed, as it turned out; he was the lead guitar player of the band I had rocked to all day. He asked my name, told me he had seen me dancing on the hill that day, and that I had distracted him. He cooed, *"you are so beautiful"* as he turned and walked away.

I stood there dumb, numb and speechless, as I watched him stroll away. The man I loved just sauntered right out of my life. What was happening, I asked myself. How he could just walk away from everything, I felt between us. After all, in a heartbeat, I knew this man was my soulmate, my destiny. Three days later, he called. He'd gone out of his way to find me. It doesn't get any more romantic than that – much more magical than asking me for my number. Who does that? Rock stars do that.

We fell in love. We were a matched set, a man and a woman who shared a creative, artistic sensitivity. We marveled at finding each other. We were so much alike in our ways that it was easy to be vulnerable and delicate too, until we recognized we had the same heart, the same mind, about the rules of engagement. He called every night, at 8:00 sharp. Every evening, I felt closer to him than the evening before. It was bliss, until he fell over the edge, like the energizer bunny, when I had not realized there was an edge, or that he was the bunny. I should have known, should have seen the signs, but I did not. We never got drunk together. We had a glass, maybe two, with a meal, but that was it. I never saw him hammered.

THE MOCKTAIL: Bliss in a Glass
1 1/2 oz. coconut milk
3/4 oz. cream
2 oz. pineapple juice
3/4 oz. banana syrup
1 banana
Shake well over ice in a Mocktail Shaker!
 Strain and fill with crushed ice.
Top with banana slices, and share.
Stemware: Collins Glass

The only time I saw him crocked was on New Year's Eve. He sent a car to Russian Hill, as a regular routine, to deliver me to Marin. He always met the car and told the driver a funny story. But this night, I was a few hours late. No lights were on, no handsome funny Latin man greeted my car. I found my way to the door and knocked. The man who greeted me was not the man I knew, at all. We went out for dinner as planned, but he could barely eat two bites. He slammed down martinis and got totally wasted. For the first time ever, I saw him inebriated.

We went home to his place, popped a bottle of bubbly, took a sip to toast the New Year and went directly to bed. He held me and spoke softly to me in Spanish of his love for me, and for us. I could not concentrate on his words for all the noise going on inside my head.

I later sneaked into the living room to let the seriousness of his condition sink in on a real level. I was in love with a drunk again. As I sat in the stillness of the night, I came

My love called later in the day and told me he did not want me to see him in that condition. It was the night before he went into an in-patient, alcohol rehab center. He told me how much he loved me, said that we were soulmates and that we belonged together. He asked if I believed in destiny. I said, *"Sometimes destiny gets screwed up."* Why did I say that? Why did I fail to speak my heart? The man poured his heart out; his words flowed like water that night. I couldn't speak. I couldn't utter a single coherent word. I wanted to change the subject as if it was all a nightmare. I was so shocked to learn that he was a real alcoholic and would be in a treatment program, for what he said would be the better part of a year. I was mute, frozen with pain. Before I could gather myself together, to think to speak, he whispered, *"I never heard you tell me you loved me."* With those final words, he hung up.

I tried in vain to call him back, no answer, nothing. I went to the cabinet and threw what liquor I had away and did what anyone would do, whose love was in a rehabilitation center God knows where. I painted huge flowers all over the refrigerator and on the windows, as I waited to hear from him. I sat at the big bay window overlooking the San Francisco Bay, seeing nothing, feeling numb, and fretful.

I waited. Days crept into sleepless nights, it felt like forever, but I knew we would be together again. When he got out, it was our destiny. He had asked me to wait for him, and I said I would. We did not need to drink alcohol. The times we spent together without drinking were much sweeter. A few weeks later, he called from the pay phone in the rehab center and told me not to wait for him. I sobbed, *"But I do love you."* I cried and he cried. We never spoke again. My world got broken that day. I guess I sort of cyber-stalked him for a while after that. No that is a bold-faced lie. I did cyber-stalk his site, like a junkie needing a fix. I hit that page several times a day, just to get a heady taste, of his face, it was a lot, addiction, but eventually, I snapped out of it. I think of him soberly, somberly now. I still have that picture of him, Carlos Santana and Lou Rawls hanging on my wall. It is a one-of-a-kind, it always was.

THE MOCKTAIL: California Smooth
7 large strawberries
8 oz. lemon yogurt
1/3 cup orange juice
Place strawberries in a plastic container and freeze for about an hour or just use frozen strawberries! Blend the frozen strawberries, yogurt, and orange juice until smooth, *real smooth*.

Stemware: Collins Glass

Do these stories resonate with your life experience? Have you encountered a person that you know was destined to be in your life, to have it all evaporate? The *"Angels Share"* I suspect that love goes to the guardian angels.

Love feelings can also become an addiction. I guess that is why people, who have been through a treatment program, must abstain from a serious love connection, for the better part of a year. They find themselves in a supporting community; they do their recovery work and do not take another taste of *anything* that would trigger the loss of their sobriety. Just one taste could tip them over the edge, like the energizer bunny. Have you ever been the bunny? The kind that tips over the edge, I mean. I have not, although seeing the one I loved tip over, felt like I had tipped over too.

Mending takes time, not just for the bunny, for those who loved the bunny.

14: Hanging it Up - Bottoms Up

"I only got a toilet seat cushion so my face would be comfortable after an intense night of drinking"
- anonymous

Booze, booze, booze, buzz; Recognition-Realization-Rumination-booze is not your friend. A few popular misconceptions:

- Your heart is broken; guess you will get some booze. *Booze does not mend your heart.*

- When you are lit, you are never sexier. *Actually, projectile barfing before you have sex or stumbling across the living room into the boudoir is not sexy. Booze does not make you sexy.*

- Booze brings out your irresistible sense of humor, and witty repertoire, you are a virtual dream. *In reality, the man, who initially thought you were his dream girl, discovers you are his worst nightmare.*

- Booze makes you funny. You are so hilarious that you can hardly stand it. *Trust me, you are not funny, nobody can stand it. Booze does not make you funny.*

- If you stand while drinking booze, you will not get drunk so fast. *Sit down girl you are tripping.*

- Drinking wine is not like drinking actual alcohol, even children in Europe drink wine with dinner. You are of European ancestry. *Good for you, wine is still alcohol honey.*

- You don't drink alone so you're not an alcoholic. *Your problem is you're rarely alone, right? It's 2:00 in the afternoon and your friend says 'want a cocktail?' You say, it's only 2 and your friend says "it's 5 somewhere." You laugh and say ok just one.*

- You're not an alcoholic. You can handle booze. *You make excuses for why you're tipsy. You've not eaten all day, shouldn't have had that one cocktail. You're on allergy medication, anti-depressants; that last cocktail is what did it. You say, ok just one more, several times, before you call it a night.*

- You will never do this again. *Right, until you do it the next time.*

- You do not have a drinking problem. *Hell no, you are magnificent at it, no problem whatsoever, you have been practicing for decades.*

- Oh let's just get a bottle, it's cheaper that way. Let's have this lemon drop before we go out to our dinner at the finest places in Carmel. Just chug it! That's how it's done. *You knew you were slammed the minute that bomb hit your stomach. It was instant brain freeze, but you were with friends you had to carry on, and carry on you did. Who started that ridiculous rumor about me you ask? Oh never mind, it was me you say! Isn't that a stitch?*

THE MOCKTAIL: End Wrench
1 cup orange juice
1 cup tonic water
A lot of ice

Like a screwdriver without the booze and without getting totally screwed! Drink one when you feel all wrenched out of shape!

I was discovering that '*The One*' I'd called in, was not the one. I saw the folly of it all. I realized what I wanted was the real deal and virtual dating and mating was as far from real life as it could get for a woman like me. That did it for me, I quit. We French are known for that!

I decided it was time to take a good long look in the mirror. As I looked for a terribly uncomfortable length of time, I saw the real me and looking deeper, an image of a 21-year-old co-ed who was still pulling my heart strings as if I was a marionette she played with, as she watched me dance.

No matter what age you are, the child in you plays.

My child wanted to play dress up and make believe and live a glamorous social life, drinking pretty drinks poured into beautiful stemware. The suave partner looks lovingly into my eyes, we hold hands, and talk about nothing at all as the sun sets over the deep blue sea. The book '*Calling in the One*', is really about calling in your own authentic self first, at least, that's what I have come to believe.

I attract and am attracted to alcoholics because I had a drinking '*issue.*' Let's not call it a problem, as that is so unattractive. I had to dig down to the core issue that I drank to make-believe. Once into a make-believe situation for a year or so, the reality eventually wins out. Then I come out of the make-believe world and wake up to the fact that I was with another alcoholic.

Usually, I was the one who realized that my chosen partner had a serious problem with alcohol or drugs or both and I did not want to be around it any longer. I would end the relationship the play was over, close the curtain. No encore, don't take a bow, just hit the road. *Alcoholics are actually attractive people in the short run, but not for the long haul.*

The thing is I could go for months and years without drinking alcohol at all. I had successfully mocked repeatedly. Then a new man came along and I would have a drink again. I honestly have loved a couple of men in my life, and I will always love them in my own way. *I do not have the love switch off valve, but my lush light has an automatic pilot.*

I know that alcohol did nothing to help us go the distance. In truth, it kept a barrier between us. A grown woman, yet I put the co-ed in charge of my dating and mating scene. I did not know how to engage in a real-life love situation, without the classic cocktail in hand. *I can go years between love stories and cocktails.*

Titillating Facts on Women, Alcohol, and Sex:

A study was conducted to determine how many women drink alcohol before having sex. More than 3,000 women were surveyed and four out of 10 say they have 'always' been a bit tipsy when they have slept with a partner for the first time. Yes, sure, a bit tipsy could be falling down drunk, but let's just call it tipsy.

Ladies, do you think guys know that nearly half, 48.5 percent said they preferred sex while under the influence? Do you think knowing that would deflate the male ego just a tiny bit? Three-quarters of women in the sample study claimed they felt more able to let their hair down and go wild after a few drinks. No kidding? Did we truly need a *study* to confirm that alcohol helps one let their hair down and loosens one up to do things that they might not do otherwise?

Here is the real ball buster, 75 percent of women said they liked to drink before having sex with their husband or boyfriend! Do you think 75 percent of men need to drink to have sex with their wife or girlfriend? Seriously, I believe that they can pretty much do it sober, and actually, they do a better job of it when they are not toasted. Only six per cent of women have never had sex while sober. Yeah, that is probably a small number. I will bet a bottle of B & B that number is a lot higher than six per cent. It was also revealed that 14 per cent of women in a relationship can't face having sex with their partner unless they had a couple of glasses of wine beforehand. What, does the partner know she can't face having sex with him without the wine? Notice they say it is wine. What about morning sex, they don't have a bottle hidden under the bed do they?

British women say they have on average 8 sexual partners and they report that they were drunk when they had sex with five of them and couldn't remember the names of 2 of the guys the next morning; so, what about that 1 lone guy where does he fit into the equation; just curious. A whopping five out of 10 chicks prefer drunken sex to sober sex. What they are saying here is that half of the women polled prefer, want, need, *must* be drunk to make whoopie!

American women claim to have an average of nine sexual partners, but the gals that rack up the most numbers in the sack are the chicks from New Zealand where they average about 20 sexual partners. That is the down low on the down under.

Could be the New Zealand women are just telling it like it is while the Brits and the Yanks like to sound less adventurous; these are self-reported statistics. Maybe millions of couples around the globe, and tri-zillions of couples in New Zealand all have to get a little bombed before they have sex together!

Women are drinking alcohol like fish, just to swim with the sharks it seems.

A professor at the University of North Dakota spent 20 years studying the drinking habits of women. Dr. Wilsnack notes that women are not drinking a lot more than they ever did but they are getting more intoxicated, inebriated, toasted, or sloshed on purpose. That is correct: Women today are drinking more intentionally to get blasted.

Robert Hess said it best, *"Isn't drinking just to get drunk a lot like having sex just to get pregnant?"*

THE MOCKTAIL: Virgin Hot Sex

2 oz. triple sec
4 oz. orange juice
1 dash grenadine syrup
Fill a highball glass with ice. Add triple sec.
Drizzle the grenadine syrup over the ice.
Add orange juice and stir
Garnish with a flower – isn't that sweet?

Co-eds cuties have been chugging and slamming drinks forever. Today there are sassier names for getting ripped quickly, what used to known as binge drinking is now called 'pregamming' or 'frontloading' where women drink on average four drinks consecutively to the male counterpart of five.

My own alma mater and university where I was an adjunct, has their own girlie brand of pregamming, according to Ms. Saunders, age 21. *"My friends will fill up a water bottle with vodka — one bottle is a little less than half a fifth — and take it with them when they go out. It'll be gone by the end of the night."*

Notice that Ms. Saunders has friends who do this and she's just an innocent bystander, sort of a reporter on campus life, kind of gal. I think I know her uncle. *Go Chips!*

THE MOCKTAIL: College Punch
2 quarts pineapple juice
2 quarts apple juice
2 quarts orange juice
1 quart ginger ale
1 quart orange Sorbet
Garnish, strawberries!

Combine and mix all ingredients in a very cool container and have fun, go chips!

Stemware: Really? Use the plastic throw- away cups for this!

What I came to realize, is that my issue was alcohol and not just the alcohol, but what they poured the drink into, that fabulous sexy stemware. I had come to the tipping point. The point that makes a difference in the course of events and for me, the course I would take to live right out loud. That was it.

After a string of alcoholics, plus my own propensity toward being the occasional lush, I looked for a way to continue my life, without all that downside. That is when I truly became *the* original Mock Star.

My mock will get the biggest test when a man's presence makes my heart sing and my spirits dance again. Will I have the courage to be me? I do believe I may have to date younger men again. I think we all should date younger men until '*The One*' comes along. I am not sure I truly mean that statement. I just like how it sounds.

Trust me I am fully aware that the study I just laid on you, about the sexual habits of women, is not exactly a big selling point on having Mocktails instead of wine!

Yet, with both loves of my life, stone cold sober sex holds deep meaning for me. We seemed to be wearing smiles on our faces, most of the time, and it had nothing to do with drinking alcohol, none what so ever. Therefore, that study does not blow my mind. I am not worried about it in the slightest.

It just takes the right man, ladies.

One should not have to be blitzed to make love to a man she loves. I am getting a group of Mock Stars together, so we can share our stories of authenticity and stone cold sober lovemaking.

We will need a cohort study on this one. *Yes, women do love to talk about sex.* The big question, though, will my next true love be an alcoholic. The short answer is no!

I am thinking of having business cards printed to give to the man who immediately takes my breath away, who makes my heart sing and my Kundalini spirits dance, the card will read: *I find you very attractive. Please seek help for your alcohol issue immediately. Call me as soon as you get out, ok? 800-YOU-ROCK*

15: Should You Consider Mocking?

"Reality is an illusion created by a lack of alcohol."
- N.F. Simpson

Mocking may or may not be something you are interested in for yourself.

However, if you have gotten this far through *Party like a Mock Star!,* something tells me you are seriously considering the benefits, the daring change in your lifestyle and in the way you look and feel.

You're thinking of how you will dare to be real and date and mate and have a blast partying with no regrets Mocktails!

Before you vote the idea up or down, scroll through the list below and see how many reasons to drink alcohol you can call your own:

- To go with the flow
- To fit in with the coolest girls in school-town-club-social circle
- To fit in with the big dogs the bad boys
- To fit in at all
- To be accepted
- To disrespect the rules
- To not be invisible
- To be happy when you are sad inside

- To get high because reality really stinks
- To look glamorous like the ads
- To get noticed like the stars in the tabloids
- To get over lost love
- To feel in love
- To feel sexy
- To have sex
- To get loose and let your hair down
- To get out of your mind and into your body
- To feel grown-up
- To feel anything
- To feel nothing
- To numb out
- To tune in at a party
- To tune out life's static
- To have fun like they do in the movies
- To have something to alter your ego
- To have something to make the person you are with more interesting
- To have something to make you more interesting
- To have something to alter your perception of life's tragedies
- To make believe
- To wear a mask

Does answering yes to any of the items on the previous list make you an alcoholic? I don't know, are you? Do you think you have an issue with drinking alcohol? Did you wind up with a great pair, of alcoholic genetic markers? Did many people in your extended family become full-blown alcoholics? Do you have blackout episodes or the constant need to find an excuse for why you were wasted? Do you often feel ashamed of the way you behaved while drinking? Do you feel you are super cool because you can drink with the best of them? There are tons of online tests to help you determine your professional drinking status. Take one, two, a dozen and see how it all shakes out.

Actually, the outcome to the quizzes does not amount to a shot of whiskey if you have determined that partying is the way to go for you. Do as you will – no one can walk in another's very cute Manolo Blahnik heels, no one can ask, plead or demand, that you live your life one way or another it is your choice and it always has been.

It all comes down to the life you are living, how you feel and your state of happiness. As Billy Crystal once said, *"it's not how you feel it's how you look darling"* and looking good is great, but when you feel great, you look even better.

It is my intention to make a difference in my life, because the way I had been living, was not giving me the outcomes I desired.

Are you achieving the desired results in your life? Are you fulfilling your destiny? If you are not living it the way you dreamt it would be, you might consider taking a good long uncomfortable look in the mirror.

You may take into account joining the growing numbers of Mocktail Cuties who are gracing the halls at events everywhere right now. Yes, they have infiltrated your party scene! So much so, that there are articles about the

Mocktail movement literally taking over the traditional cocktail scene.

I truly did LOL, when reading a recent article in Grub Tree, written by Chris Crowley. I love his tongue-in-cheek take, on the growing popularity of Mocktail happy hours. He is incensed, that they are so over-the-top that they are threatening to take over the entire New York, Los Angeles, Austin and London cocktail scenes! Imagine that, putting cocktail places in a dither!

The writer insists that hordes of no-booze, happy-hour seekers are what doing what he calls *"juice crawls"* all over New York. Apparently, a handful of new establishments in these four cited cities are planning Mocktail happy-hours too; which ostensibly, Crowley, believes is akin to the prohibition era without the mandate or the sanity. Hilarious! Three of the largest cities in the world (and Austin, which may be smaller, but the stars grow bright, deep in the heart of big old Texas!) are trending rapidly toward a Mocktail happy hour! Excellent news, to those of us who love Mocktail happy-hour!

There are still many places you cannot get a Mocktail, despite Crowley's lament. The kick you seek, the smooth rich fullness, and the delightful fruit layers, served up in the sexy stemware and finished off with the perfect, delectable garnish or the tiny umbrella sans booze is not always easy to find. The article does go on to mention, the *"amazement by how much clarity people say they have when sober, compared to when they are very drunk!"* What a wonderful way to advertise to everyone, that there is a Mocktail movement underway. In a few of the largest cities in the world and Austin, there are bunches of very savvy people stepping up with an aim to step out for Mocktail happy hour. They want to have zippy- zero-proof drinks and get happy, just like everybody else in the City!

16: Rock the Mock!

Being sober on a bus is, like, totally different than being drunk on a bus
- Ozzy Osbourne

How do you rock your mock? Mocking, simplified, is *drinking* – there is just no alcohol.

You have a drink in your hands, hopefully in a beautifully shaped glass, and maybe even an umbrella or sprig of celery to boot, but the drink you're sipping is only 'mocking' an actual drink.

You can drink to your heart's content but there is no chance you are going to end up dancing on tabletops or wearing the proverbial lampshade.

It can be an incredible change.

I began putting some real energy into creating a perfect clone of cocktails that are indistinguishable mocks.

My mock experience started out smooth. I ran into a few bartenders that were on the wagon and could fix the best non-alcoholic drinks on the planet.

Once at a show in Mill Valley with a gaggle of my drinking, dosing gal friends.

I waited until they had their orders then sauntered over to the little bar and whispered to the bartender: *"Hey man, I am here with my girls and I need a fake cocktail that has everything in it including an umbrella."*

He smiled and motioned me closer to the side of the bar. *"I get you, girl, I have not had alcohol in years. I will mix up the fanciest and tastiest drink in town, umbrella and all. You will love it!"*

OK, this was my man!

The band was hot, so was the place, and the girls were hammered. One looked over at my 4ᵗʰ big old mocktail with an umbrella in it and said *"holy shit girl you better slow down, let me have a sip."* She took a sip then another and yelled *"oh my God you can't even taste the booze in that thing Z – you are going to be so toasted tomorrow. I think you better be cutting them off right now."*

I thanked her and then thanked the barkeep, who just gave me a big wink and said: "Doll, anytime."

Success, for me: Mocking was here to stay.

THE MOCKTAIL: Banana Cabana Colada

3 medium bananas chunked
1-cup milk
8 oz. crushed pineapple in juice
6 tbsp. cream of coconut
2 tbsp. sugar
1 1/2 tbsp. ground allspice
2 cups crushed ice

Blend, the bananas, milk, pineapple and its juice, cream of coconut, sugar and allspice until it is creamy and thick.
Add the ice and blend it, and do it again, until it is smooth.

Stemware: Big ole glass
Do not forget the umbrella

17: Don't Knock My Mock!

Well, don't knock it until you mock it, girls. It's fun! As I always say, *"Darling we aren't all Shirley Temples. Serve us hot mamas something glamorous in a very sexy glass and don't skimp on the garnish sweetheart."*

Just the other night, my friend Robin, who once worked clubs in Atlantic City, and enjoys her wine, and the occasional beer, invited me out for Mocktails after work. I was so surprised and glad to share in her virgin run in the Mocktail scene.

We stopped in at the Rainbow on the Sunset Strip and had a Mocktail, the ever popular, Faux Cosmo. We had some food, chatted it up over the din of the World Series and she confided *"that was excellent; I have no craving for alcohol Z that was very cool."* Thank you, Rainbow room for making us a gigantic, and superb Mocktail! Stop by the Sunset Strip, and get your own big taste of the Rainbow!

Mocking is the *easy* way to change your relationship with alcohol, with yourself and others.

Mocktail drinking enables you in coping with the expectations, norms, professional and social pressure, to partake in drinking alcohol. The art of mocking is simply doing the same things you have always enjoyed doing, but choosing to take part in them, in a different manner. It's ladies choice. A new way of experiencing life is at hand. In this case, it is *in* hand.

The *hard* way would be to cut off drinking anything that even remotely resembles an alcoholic drink. This guide is for the woman who is fully conscious of the fact, that she is capable of handling alcohol, some of the time, but not all of the time, for whatever reason. Mocking in the way suggested in *Party like a Mock Star!,* allows you to keep having fun, enjoying life and creating opportunities to see life and people around you in a slightly different light. You may have missed a few special moments along the way.

THE MOCKTALE: The recipe for Mocking

1- part intelligence

2- parts practice

1-part acting

Just blend until smooth.

Not much different from when you were drinking your brains out, with just that one exclusion, alcohol.

Truth, peer pressure is alive and well at every stage in life. Some things never change and peer pressure on drinking alcohol is one of them. It is very true, that those drinking alcohol, often insist that everyone within elbow distance of them must be slamming down drinks as well. These things happen and you do not have to set yourself up for the trap! Avoid the trap, set up your attitude before you hit the door, *'I can get away with it'* the woman who can snuggle up to the bar in an elegant establishment or at a club and get, what I want, the way I want it.

I am of the school, that it's not something you confess and it's how the Mocktail got its name. It ain't nobody's business but your own. So play this Taj tune before you leave the house *"It Ain't Nobody's Business But My Own!"* Of course, that song is laced with lots of jive talk about drinking, but it's a fun tune and it gets your head ready to make Mocking your own business!

Life can be such an illusion. Having a degree of poise, however, is not. You will still light up a room, but not with outrageous behaviors. This speaks volumes of your own self-worth, as a human being. You know how to engage with others of any station, at any type of function and know the precise time to leave. Knowing when to take off is key!

THE MOCKTAIL: Classy Coconut
4 oz. pineapple juice
1 oz. crème de coconut
1 splash cranberry juice
2 oz. Grenadine syrup
1 oz. cherry juice

Cherry garnish
Put some ice in your Mocktail shaker
Pour entire contents and shake it up
Garnish: Wild Card

It took a long while to understand the psychology of why I drank and longer still to understand the way in which drinking alcohol had woven itself into the fabric of my life. I decided to repurpose the fabric and see what I could make out of it. I still absolutely need to have fun, party, and dance, but I intend to do it sober.

I love my life, my family and myself and perhaps I may find that I will love a man again. I am seriously embarrassed that I put myself through the online dating madness and have the courage to write about it.

I am quite confident I would enjoy a relationship with a man of substance again, but not for marriage. To that point, A University of Cincinnati study found that married women actually drink slightly *more* than their single counterparts do. Who needs another reason to drink, I mean really!!

I am sure that all I actually want is a weekend husband.

By husband, I mean a man I will love, who loves me back. We will be monogamous, live in our separate dwellings and get together on the weekends, for special events, holidays, trips, and live happily ever after. *"It's never too late to fall in love. It's never too late to wink an eye. I will do it until the day I die...the, boyfriend."* I did that play! That is how I would like my song to end.

A very appealing man, applied for the position awhile back because I said precisely that, *"Oh I am just looking for a weekend husband."* He liked that, and he liked the fact that I had told him I was his date for the evening, twenty minutes after making his acquaintance, just for the pure novelty of saying such an outrageous thing, sober.

We had a particular, Je ne sais pas, a certain chemistry. Yet, it was a bit awkward for me, as I had not one single cocktail in my system, although neither, did he.

He was a passionate kisser; smearing my red lipstick all over both of our faces, he was a passionate Italian. He was definitely a man of experience and in my mind; he was the real life version of the most interesting man in the world, except he was not hawking beer.

Later, I sent him a photo taken from that evening and he answered, *"See what happens when you employ your angels and make that leap."*

It was a big leap for me, no hooch, straight on me. It felt odd, yet good all at the same time, just a little taste of freedom. An experience without alcohol, just a hint of coconut, it just was an attraction, a one big kiss wonder with the magic man.

THE MOCKTAIL: Coconut Lips
2 oz. pineapple juice
1 1/2 oz. cream
1/4 - 3/4 oz. coconut cream
1/4 oz. raspberry syrup
Shake well over ice cubes in a Mocktail shaker.
Strain over crushed ice
Garnish with a pineapple hunk, oops, I mean chunk and an umbrella!

Stemware: Highball Glass

It is my mission to guide and influence women on their path toward Mock Stardom! Cheers to you, you all deserve the freedom to be Mock Stars!

Stone Cold Sober is Hot!

What is so hot about being sober you ask? For starters you are. Then, let us recall the magic man; he was a stone cold sober male with the unmistakable air of the most interesting man in the world.

Here are a few more reasons I believe sober it is hot. If you are not going out to a bar to catch a cocktail on a first date, you will have some other fun, and an original date planned. What's hot is hot! Maybe you go to a sporting event, watch a pro basketball or football team if you are into that. I am and I think that is a hot date!

Perhaps you go to a fantastic concert where you dance your brains out and cannot have a drink on the dance floor. I am into that and the date gets massive extra hot points for being able to dance! Perhaps you go to an observatory and watch the stars together, that is romantic and that is hot. There are many options and who knows where this could lead? Roller derbies, horse races… stop me!

Being engaged in a physical activity you love you are most authentic, and that is hot! Find your passion in your own life, now that truly is hot!

You have a better shot at knowing what and whom you want when you are not wasted. Did we need to say that? Yes, that is why we are here! This is all hot stuff girls, stoned cold sober beats tipsy, wobbly or falling down drunk any day and in every way.

I do not have to drink to be out with people who are, yet I so enjoy my Mocktails. I am a Mock Star, so I go out to places where people are having cocktails, and am often mildly amused around my friends when they're wasted but not always. The one thing I am very definite about and say with all the confidence of a real Mock Star, *"I will not date or fall in love with an alcoholic ever again. I reached that tipping point quite a while ago."*

It may have taken me an exceptionally long time to get to the tipping point, but the point is I got there. I love my life and all sorts of wonderful exciting adventures have unfolded for me as a result. I am experiencing all the rush in a state of full conscious awareness.

However, before you begin Mocking, you still may have some questions.

Does mocking make me a poser?

Yes. You are drinking Mocktails so that people do not exert undue pressure on you to have a cocktail. Some people do that out there, meaning at your business after hours, networking, political events, casual meetings and socializing, and you may know a few of them. You do not confess your mocking unless caught *in flagrante delicto,* less formally that is to say, with your pants down. People simply cannot handle it. I am not sure if it makes them feel like you have an incurable contractible disease or if it just brings their own issues up, so they leave you behind like roadkill to find people they perceive will be more fun. You *are* fun. You *are* charming. If posing with a Mocktail at a gathering allows you to mingle and have fun, then no harm, no foul.

Does mocking make a mockery of my authenticity?

"Be yourself; everyone else is already taken."
– Oscar Wilde

Long Answer: Do you have yourself all figured out? Did you take three or four different personality profile courses to discover that each and every test you took the results all indicate, that you are a social interactor, a dominate director, or a steady relator? Does knowing how you rank in a personality indicator give you a real gauge of your authentic self? Have you worked with astrology, numerology, and spiritual leaders to come to a greater understanding of your authenticity? Are you fire, water, air, or wind sign; are you a snake, a rabbit, or a dragon guided daily by the stars alignment? Do you follow a spiritual path that is not a contradiction of your real self? Do you meditate to find your true self? Have you been brainwashed into who you are? Does a record play in your mind that influences your sense of self?

Did you know that when you meet three or four different people at the same time, that most likely each one of them will have a different perception of you for all they see is your mask? Some people claim that they do not wear a mask, that what you see is what you get. I do not know if that is true. I believe everyone wears a mask lots of time consciously or unconsciously.

When does your real self just come bursting out? What calls to you? What is your passion in life? That passion that involves *only* you; like playing an instrument, running for miles, traveling, singing, painting, dancing, what is it you have a passion for that makes you feel like a ten even if the day has been a two? When was the last time you engaged in your passion?

My passion, my story: I recall when teaching hours of dance each day, that I was in my pure heart and mind. The hours I spent with music, the movement was the one place and activity that made me happy, no matter what else may be happening around me. I am my true self then. Nothing can alter that feeling.

Also, on those rare and incredibly moving occasions, when dancing, I would go into another dimension and become the dance, no longer the dancer. When I came back from wherever it was I knew that I had been one with the universe. In those moments, I was right with the world.

What makes you happy, no matter what else is happening around you? Engage in whatever *that* is every single day. Being authentic is something that you feel when your heart and your mind are harmonious and there is happiness.

I believe we are most authentic when we feel happy. Moreover, that happiness does not revolve around another human being but comes from your true self. That is my unprofessional sense of authenticity.

I also firmly believe that not drinking alcohol will be of great assistance in finding you. I think Mocking will create a space for you to follow your passion and be happy.

Short Answer: No, it will not make a mockery of your authenticity. Find your passion, do your passion every day, therein you find your authenticity.

Will he or she still love me if I mock?

"If you can stay in love for more than two years, you're on something." — Fran Lebowitz

Asking this question indicates you have confided in that certain someone that you are not drinking alcohol and that your drink looks like booze, yet is not. You do not have to tell most anyone anything unless you want to, as it is your choice. If he or she finds that a reason to not be in love with you, or is unable to continue to love you as a mocker he or she did not love you at all.

Love is a mysterious thing. There is always that slim chance that once you stop drinking cocktails and start drinking Mocktails, you will not be as in love with your mate, as when you were both drinking. You do not need another alcoholic in your life sweetheart. Love does not have to hurt to be real. *Rock your Mock!*

Will I fit in with my best alcoholic off-the-wall friends?

"This is a good place," he said. "There's a lot of liquor," I agreed.
- Ernest Hemingway

I would not share my Mocking if I were out Chelsea or friends who are Chelsea groupies. They are not on a need-to-know basis. You can show them how much you adore them by being their designated driver DD on occasion. Not every time you go out, you are not their mommy. Being a reliable DD by special request is nice, but taking care of your tipsy friends every time you go out, will become too great a burden. Do they start before they get to the club, pregamming-front loading, to be half way there before they *actually* get there? You will have a glass of something, laugh and enjoy your friends, as long as you are actually enjoying them. You will know when it is time for you to leave. Even if they throw a fuss, they will not miss you when you are out of sight, they are buzzed remember? You know you are still going to have fun, you will just do it your way. There will be a ton of new experiences. You just love new experiences. Who knows, you just may run into a fellow mocker along the way. You may decide to solicit some of your finest drinking friends to help you sample Mocktails in your city. Do a taste testing night out on the town.

Recently, I recruited a couple of friends in New Orleans, LA [NOLA] to try some Mocktails for me in the Big Easy. Jeremey and Becca Pino were delighted to give me a hand in 86ing the hooch for the sake of research and hitting a few clubs. They said, *"what great timing, we were just talking about cutting down on the booze, getting ready to take a well-deserved break. Tell us where to go and what to order and we are on it!"* You are going to get the Pino's juicy professional opinions on some of the Mocktails they tasted, later in this guide. You just might be surprised how many will follow the lead should you elect to engage a few of your friends on the hunt for the best Mocktail in your city!

How Will My Family React to My Mocking?

"I had sent her to four consecutive psychiatrists, and not one of them had gotten me sober."
– Anonymous

Do you want to mess with the family tree? In my case, I shared my Mocktail scene with my little family. My son and my daughter-in-law gave me big hugs and said right on Z. My darling daughter found out a few months later asking *"you do not drink that much anyway, so what is the big deal?"* Sometimes it is not the amount we drink or how often, it is how it makes us feel. I shared my *"Fat Tongue Syndrome"* theory with my daughter and told her someday she would remember that story and have one of those ah- ha moments. She is thrilled, said she just cannot wait! My little family and I have been out to some fabulous places all over San Francisco, Los Angeles, and Squaw Valley, for various functions and family retreats. I have to say they get right in on the action of discovering the best possible Mocktail when we are out at a fine dining establishment.

Not long ago, at Greenblatt's Deli on the strip in Los Angeles, I had the root beer that comes in a beer bottle, while the kids were drinking real beer. I had fun and it fit the scene. I honestly cannot stand beer, but holding on to that ugly bottle, slurping my root beer just worked.

In San Francisco, at a lovely little place called Fire Fly, we found some great bottled fizzy juice concoction, poured into a wine glass. It went well with my meal. I know my son and daughter-in-law thought it was kind of an adventure to help select the perfect Mocktail that evening.

While in Squaw Valley, this summer for our annual family gathering, we went to a cool little place outside of the Valley and I ordered a Ginger Beer concoction. I cannot say I loved it, or hated it either.

Everybody else, the beer drinkers in the party, took a swig and gave it two thumbs up. Therefore, I think it is an acquired taste.

The rest of the gang was drinking their fancy craft beers, debating the quality of this one over another. I am seriously mystified at how they could stand any of them.

Yet, I listened and I learned, and I tried to retain, however, the next day I forgot everything about beer and I was stone cold sober. You have to be into it. Hey, beer lovers, you will most likely enjoy a Ginger Beer!

18: Mocktail Mixing and Shaking It Up

Some believe that making a mean Mocktail is easy.

However, if you are not a professional mixologist, you are going to be stuck with some disappointing Mocktails in my opinion.

People who tell you Mocktails are just adding fruit to some tonic water do not really have what it takes to give advice.

When I first began Mocking, I must confess that was my go-to as well, although I always insisted on the exquisite stemware and the garnish to create the vision. My taste in Mocktails has seriously matured.

This guide is jammed with recipes that I've been testing-tasting for you darlings. My advice, do what you did when drinking alcohol, practice, practice, practice until you discover what brings a smile when you drink it.

Going out is always entertaining, but having guests in your home is also fun! How to DIY your Mocktail Scene: *Drinking Mocktails is something you can actually drink at home alone and not worry that you have a drinking problem.*

Mocktail 'chic' stems from pouring a little energy and thought into to the preparation to get it down! It's the right glass and garnish [we've been saying that all along] and from there it is like anything else you wish to master, practice, practice, practice until it feels right!

Awesome Mocktails do not rely solely on taste. That's what *Party like a Mock Star!* is all about! You know, it's an illusion, the look, the vibe, the whole Mocking thing!

It's visual and of course the taste, without the visual appeal, though, it totally affects the taste! Michelle and I were having a Mocktail at the Roku Sunset the other day. It was a delight to watch Charity mix it up for us, but moreover, it looked so inviting! It tasted great too; we didn't miss the booze at all.

As we were leaving, there was one of *Charity's Ginger Delights* left and we asked one of the staff if he might like it. He looked at us as if we were soused and said: *"No we aren't allowed to drink alcohol while working!"* That's how convincing this *Ginger Delight* looked. The perfect Mocktail that you will see Charity making in our *Party Like a Mock Star* video episode!

Next, we list a few basics in stemware that you should have around for your Mocktail experiences. I have collected many sets, over the years. You may have as well. This is not an all-inclusive list; it is merely a place to start for the Mocktail novice. *You may now throw away your throw-away cups.*

Just the basics:

Shot glass: Yes, you will still use the shot glass in the preparation of your Mocktail. The shot glass is for measuring purposes, but my guess is you have seen friends actually drink from them. You stood there in shock, but yes it has been done I hear. You may have a few random shot glasses around; trade them up for an attractive one!

Mixing Glass: Well, this is for mixing! Designed for times when shaking will not do. They come in all sizes to suit your style. The smaller mixing glass will also seat your strainer, keeping the concoction from going rouge on you!

Rocks Glass: The rocks glass is a straight-sided thick-bottomed tumbler to hold up to the muddling, and the rocks you push around in them. They hold between 4 and 8 ounces of Mocktail delight. It is short, sturdy design is ideal for your Mocktail, poured over ice aka as on the rocks!

Highball Glass: You are going to serve your Mocktail highball in this taller version of the rocks glass, straight sides and holds 8 to 12 ounces. This glass will get a lot of use so be sure to add them to the bar!

Martini glass aka the Cocktail glass: Be still my heart, the sexiest glass ever made. This classic is an absolute must for the Mocktail Bar. Nothing better displays a shaken or stirred cocktail. These will vary widely in size from the petite to the jumbo. Although the martini glass and cocktail glass are slightly different, use either when a recipe calls for a cocktail glass. Technically the cocktail glass has a slight curve to the rim. I prefer the martini glass and don't own any cocktail glasses and I feel fine about that! I use the medium size and have more than one!

Champagne flute: The flute is also my favorite, it's sleek and sophisticated. Use it for your mock champagne and mock Mimosas, which are actually magnificent by the way. The champagne flute typically holds 6 to 9 ounces. The tall stem has a narrow opening that keeps the bubbly sweet and bubbly. So be sure to use bubbly stuff when mixing up a batch, more on this later.

Wine glasses: The essential Mocktail bar will have both the red and the white wine glass set up. The red wine glass is wider allowing the faux wine to breathe. We are going for the vision, so you will want to use the red stemware when you have found the perfect blend for grape juice to produce the color and depth of the red you are mocking. The white wine glass is narrower to keep the white faux wine chilled. You'll have fun playing with various fruit juice and other options to create the texture, color, and Mockability of the juices. Obviously, you serve the red wine at room temperature and the white wine chilled. Keep that in mind when you mix Mocktail wines.

Collins glass: You thought you would put your Mock Collins in the highball glass didn't you? Well, that is perfectly fine and people often do. However, the exact Collins is taller and slimmer and holds 10-14 ounces of frosted perfection, perfect for any of your fizzy types of drinks like the Zoejito, the My-Tye, and others. They actually make an extra tall version of this stemware called the chimney if you need an extra tall for any reason.

Coupe glass: Many of the upscale places use the coupe to serve a martini type drink I have noticed more often of late. The breast of Marie Antoinette served as the mold in the first champagne coupe according to legend.

Seriously, I would have thought that Marie was a bit larger in that department. I do find the shape elegant and refined but actually using it for faux champagne doesn't work. The form alone lets the bubble fade far too quickly and we do not want that to happen to our Mock Bubbly!

Shake, Blend, Stir

As long as we are on it, let us talk about how the bartender or mixologist knows when to shake, blend, or stir. Bartending is for the pros. However, it might be fun to know when which is called for if you are just flying by the seat of your pants and whipping up your own artistic Mocktail.

Stirring

It's not too difficult, to stir a cocktail, but ladies, let's make it more fun: Buy a metal or glass mixing rod and mix it in your sexy mixing glass.

Muddling

In drinks like the Zoejito, you muddle, to extract the most flavors possible, from certain fresh ingredients such as fruit or mint garnishes. You crush the parts with the muddler on the back end of your bar spoon, or with a pestle, but not to the point of demolishing the garnish, you want to bruise it a bit, not kill it!

Shaking

When a recipe contains eggs, fruit juices or cream, you will shake the ingredients. Shaking is the method by which you use a Mocktail shaker, formerly known as a cocktail shaker, to mix ingredients together and to chill them at the same time.

Who knew that's why you use a Mocktail shaker! The bunch of ice cubes goes in while you pour the rest of the mix into the shaker; apparently, it's to freeze the drink, *almost.* However, the experts tell us that it is important to not to shake the drink to death. Basically, try not to kill any of your drinks, so remember: **Drink lives matter!** How do you know when you have shaken the drink sufficiently? When the shaker begins to have condensed water on the surface, your shaking is over!

Straining

Mocktail shakers are such an essential, yet so elegant. I love them. They come with a strainer built in or a hawthorn strainer, that little gadget with the handle you use to strain the drink from your sexy shaker. When a drink calls for straining, make sure you have used ice cubes, crushed ice clogs up the strainer. Serve the drink unstrained when the recipe calls for using crushed ice.

Blending

Yet another no-brainer right? Use an electric blender for combining ingredients that do not break down simply by stirring; add with other ingredients to create a smooth and ready to devour Mocktail. Sometimes a recipe will call for ice to be blended in, so that's a pretty good tip that you will be using your blender. *Note: Use lots of ice!*

Building

Now we are getting into it. When you build your Mocktail, pour the ingredients into your Mocktail stemware in a precise manner. Usually, the parts are floated on top of each other, thick to the bottom and lighter on top. Yet, occasionally, a swizzle stick is used in the glass, allowing the ingredients to be mixed.

I used to shake, blend, stir and beat the concoction to a pulp. It was booze and *hard* stuff. I just thought it could take a beating. Now that I attempt to make some exotic Mocktails at home, I had to learn that you could not just dump it all together and hope it comes out right. There is some finesse to this Mocktail-making business. Again, this is why I like the pros to do it for me.

However, I do not have my own mixologist on standby for the occasions I want to play at home and it allows my rebel out just a bit, drinking alone at home! *Drinking Mocktails is something you can actually drink at home alone and not worry that you have a drinking problem.*

Not an exhaustive list by any means, but a start to stocking ingredients for your Mocktail bar:

- Fresh lemons
- Fresh limes
- Fresh ginger
- Cinnamon sticks
- Tiny umbrellas
- Maraschino cherries

- Olives
- Tonic water
- Sparkling water
- Club soda
- Ginger ale
- Cranberry – tomato – grapefruit – grape both white and red juice
- Ginger beer
- Different types of lemon-lime sodas
- Mai tai mixer with real fruit
- Agave nectar all natural
- Simple syrup from 100% cane sugar
- Almond syrup

Your primary Mocktail Bar equipment should include:

- Mocktail shaker, formerly known as your cocktail shaker
- Ice bucket
- Bar spoons
- Muddler
- Jigger measures
- Strainer
- Ice cube trays
- Freeze some fruit in the ice cube trays to jazz up the Mocktail
- Zester

- Sharp knife

- Blender

- Your *Party Like a Mock Star* guide!

I have shared several of my favorite Mocktails with you sprinkled throughout *Party Like a Mock Star!* I hope you like them!

One of my favorites is my namesake, a spin-off from the Mojito! I always loved a good Mojito, or so I thought. When I mixed them up for guests at my home in the past, I used Sapphire® instead of rum.

I went through tons of my fresh mint growing in the front yard and a quite a few of those huge big blue bottles of Sapphire®, mixing my legendary Mojitos up for a house full of guests. People could not get enough of them.

When I ran out of the Sapphire®, I asked my friend to go and grab a couple more big bottles because guests still wanted more of my fabulous Mojitos.

My friend looked at me with a big smirk on his face, well ok, he was out and out laughing and asked: *"Didn't you know that you make a Mojito with rum?"* Who knew?

All of us were half in the bag or perhaps all of us were completely in the bag, because the next thing you know, we are online, writing to the Sapphire® people about the fabulous new drink we just invented named the *Zoejito.*

Certainly, this new drink discovery would just have their advertising people pounding at our door, at least answering our emails, for an interview or something. Oddly, they never bothered to write us back.

We all semi-desperately wanted to like the Mojito with rum but alas, Sapphire® trumped rum at my house.

Now, not actually loving a real Mojito, as much as the Sapphire® one, which I was wild for, I can tell you that this recipe is just as good as my original *Zoejito* minus the Sapphire®!

Try it – you'll like it!

Zoejito

Mock Mojito

Serves [1]

- 8 fresh mint leaves
- ½ tsp. of fine sugar
- 1-2 medium size limes
- ½ oz. of simple syrup
- Club Soda
- Ice

You do not shake or stir actually you muddle. Place the fresh mint leaves in the bottom of a sturdy glass. Pour a little sugar and a tiny bit of lime juice on the fresh mint leaves. Press the leaves gently with a wooden spoon, or a muddle. You do not want the mint leaves to get too smashed or they become bitter; don't kill them!

Stop when you smell mint, or when the leaves begin to tear.

The leaves should remain whole, crumpled and maybe with a few tears. The purpose of muddling is to release the fragrant and tasty oils in the leaves, and roughing them up a bit will allow them to seep out and infuse your drink. Muddling the leaves with sugar will allow the oils to seep into the sugar, adding more depth to the drink.

Fill the glass with ice and the rest of the way with club soda.

Garnish with a remaining sprig of mint. Add a little more simple syrup if your Zoejito is too bitter.

Mocktails Parties

Do we need to tell you the queen of party city how to host a Mocktail Party? Apparently, we thought it was a good idea.

It's all about the presentation, the table setting, the stemware, the garnish, the ambiance, and the theme.

The introduction and serving of everything at your Mocktail party are matter of importance.

Themes are always great, as they help you set the mood for the type of food, the kind of table settings and stemware required for the accompanying Mocktails.

Give serious consideration to the stemware and the garnish for starters, there is where the Mocktail scheme gets it vibe, that and great recipes and of course according to your *Party Like a Mock Star*! Mock Star!

I dig the Madmen era Mocktail parties.

I do not tell guests it is a theme party, but it certainly is a theme party for me.

I throw on a great pair of bells and a groovy sexy top to get in the mood.

If I am hosting it by the pool, I drape a 1960s psychedelic tablecloth over the table; passed Hors d'oeuvres and have lovely trays of food on the side tables.

If this shindig is going to be inside, go with tasteful table settings and simple yet elegant decorations for the Madmen theme.

I typically opt for an oversize hurricane vase, filled with orchids or white lilies, both present well.

Mocktails for this gathering are going to focus on various martini style drinks, and possibly a gin fizz or bogus bubbly type concoction.

You will be getting out your shaker, the martini glasses, the flutes, and highball or rock glasses for this gathering.

If you are going for a Sangria taco type party, you will need to change the table setting, to create the feeling of the south of the border, *naturally*.

I use a colorful serape on the table. Fiesta styled table settings and colorful stemware.

Mix up a big beautiful bowl of Mock Sangria and if inviting drinking friends mix up another pitcher of the real deal.

Various holidays and events also create their own theme and you will simply play off the weekend, for example, throwing an Independence Day cocktail party. This one may take on more of a pool or garden setting; the table settings according to the traditional red, white and blue.

Your Mocktails will be on the cooler side, fruity with all the zing without the sting. It is your *Fauxth of July Mocktail Party!* You have this.

We know you are a pro at both attending and hosting parties. All you are doing is mixing in the Mocktail and boom baby boom a Mock Star is born.

Tip: Just as you enjoy a hostess thinking about having something more than a soda or sparkling water for the non-drinkers; remember to have the cocktail ingredients for those who still imbibe.

We want everyone to have a fabulous time at your function!

19: DIY Mocktails

Throughout this guide, I've shared some of my favorite Mocktail recipes. You can make them at home or know how to order them when you are out. The places probably won't have that 'name' that's been assigned to them, so you just have to remember what went into making them!

There's something a bit decadent if drinking such boozy type drinks at home alone, watching one your favorite shows. It's dazzling to order them when out with friends. Now you have the juice on how to order on the sly.

Here are a few more from the vault:

Another spin on the Bloody Mary this one really spices it up with the Tabasco® sauce! My cousin Kevin, from Texas, takes his Tabasco® sauce with him on trips where folks just might not have it! I've had the Virgin Bull a few times, and I like it! I use beef bouillon cubes to make them and squeeze my own lemon juice, and throw a stalk of celery into the glass as a garnish that makes it, no bull!

THE MOCKTAIL: Bloody Virgin Bull

2 oz. tomato juice
2 oz. beef bouillon
1/4 oz. lemon juice
Worcestershire sauce
Tabasco sauce
celery salt
pepper
Celery stalk

Pour tomato juice, bouillon and lemon juice over ice cubes; add sauces, salt, and pepper to taste.

Stemware: Highball or Collins glass.

"After midnight, we're gonna let it all hang down..."
- Eric Clapton

THE MOCKTAIL: Almond Midnight

2 tsp. instant coffee or a little real coffee if you want
1 glass of cold milk; you can use Almond Milk or other
types of milk to suit your soul; I like it with Almond Milk
2 tsp. instant cocoa
1 dash cream – optional- it's the calories honey
Add coffee and cocoa to milk. Add cream if you want it!

Stemware: Highball Glass

This Daiquiri clone is a very pleasant tasting and good-looking drink, you are going to look hot drinking this one!

Virgin Strawberry Daiquiri

3 oz. strawberry puree – use frozen strawberries and puree
them yourself unless you are lucky enough to find the
puree!
2 oz. pineapple juice
1/2 oz. lemon juice – fresh squeezed is super!
1 tsp confectioners' sugar
1/2 oz. strawberry syrup

Stir briefly with half a glassful of crushed ice in a wine
goblet. Garnish with strawberries or switch this all up to a
raspberry or a Blueberry Daiquiri by just swapping out the
fruit ingredients – so ingenious!

Stemware: Wine glass

"A well'a bless my soul. What's a wrong with me?...I'm in love. I'm all shook up; Mm mm mm, mm, yay, yay, yay..."
- Elvis

THE MOCKTAIL: All Shook Up

4 oz. orange juice – fresh squeezed is marvelous
1 oz. cranberry juice – go for the organic
1 egg white
1/2 tsp grenadine syrup

Shake the orange juice, cranberry juice, egg and grenadine in your Mocktail shaker, which you have half filled with ice cubes. Strain into a Rocks Glass on the rocks!

Cheers to Beers

A man named Michael wanted to hear about some darn good zero-proof beer. So what do you know, when we searched the world over and we found what beer drinkers claim to be the best options on the planet. Actually, we only found one that is zero-proof, the others are almost zero-proof, which is like being almost, *(well there are so many options to finish this thought just use the descriptor that you like best)*. It was a tough search! I am not qualified to be a judge of the taste and texture going down because even when I drank alcohol I did not drink beer. I have said that I do not fancy beer. Actually, I said I hate beer, but this is not all about me, so for you Mocktail cuties who like the taste of a good cold beer- here:

Bitburger Drive 0.0%

Bitburger Brauerei, Bitburg, Germany = 0% ABV

According to those in the know, Bitburger Drive is a German pilsner-style beer with actually no alcohol – zero-per cent. That is true beer lovers; the Bitburger Drive is zero 0.0%. The taste-testers claim this brew has a crisp, clean, and full-flavored effervescing quality, with a grassy bitter hops finish. The brewery advertises as a post-workout libation! Hip-hip; it's a Mock Beer we can hawk.

A lot of the other non-alcohol beers noted in my research has about 0.5% alcohol content in them. According to the beer experts, it is tough to distil the alcohol content from a beer and have it taste anything like beer! However, at that content, it's practically the same content of alcohol that you find in your mouthwash! Naturally, you just swish that around in your mouth, try hard not to swallow it, and then spit it out. Well, the reviews I read about non-alcohol beers said that is precisely what they wanted to do with the non-alcohol beer swish it around and spit it out for sure! These taste testers aren't novice beer drinkers apparently, and those were not their exact words.

The words they used to describe the taste of the non-alcoholic beer are: "personally insulted, makes me feel like an asshole in a very polite way, boring, pretty gross, bland, smells nasty, smells like dirty pasta water, hated it." They just didn't hold back! The people were reviewing a variety of beers for Gizmodo's weekly Booze Column, you can check it out online and see which beers got those tasty choice words! Good luck on finding a suitable non-alcoholic brewski, beer drinkers! (Michael says non-alcoholic Becks beer is acceptable though still not great).

Note: I substitute zero percent root beer in a dandy looking beer bottle, when I feel the need to drink a brewski Mocktail. When you drink it straight from the brown bottle, you look exactly like a beer drinker, *pretty much.*

If the root beer doesn't come in an excellent beer bottle, with a proper beer-type label on it, I don't waste my time trying to Mocktail it; or peel the label off from it like we all did when we were young. No, I will pour that root beer into a heavily frosted beer mug and chug a lug.

figured he would not be there at all. Turns out, he was "Special Guest" on one of the bills. It was awkward for a minute. We hugged. We both talked, but did not say much. He said he had to go check on his equipment and he would be right back. Did I panic, be right back? I flipped out.

I went and told my tripped-out girl that I was going up front for a while. I did, yet my heart was racing a mile a minute I was practically hyperventilating. Then I knew I had to bolt. I had to run away. Therefore, I did and out of the corner of my eye, I saw him standing there with his arms out as if to ask, *"Where are you going, what is going on?"* I just kept going and going I could not stop.

I did not have the courage. I practically ran home and wrote a story about the entire experience. I could not face the music, literally.

Yet another, music related Mock Tale; notice a rock mock theme here?

I was at the Doheny Blues Festival, backstage. I only go to gigs backstage. It is too much of a zoo in front. If you are young and love the field of people all doing their thing, I do not knock it, it's just not my scene anymore.

A few years back I had the obligatory two-drink ticket and wristband for backstage people and was in line for a soft drink. I waited in line with the alcohol drinkers and right through the middle of the line rode a beach cop on a standup moped.

It was so funny to me, I laughed out loud and said to no one in particular, *"Look, it's Paul Bluth Blues Fest Cop!"*

The guy behind me got it and started laughing. He took a picture of the blues fest cop, as it turns out he is a rock photographer. He had been one of Stevie Ray Vaughn's photographers back in the day.

I was not using my drink tickets so I asked the photographer if he wanted mine and we became instant friends. We are still friends and I just happen to own one of his most excellent autographed photos of Stevie Ray Vaughn, which also hangs on my wall.

Mock Tale: Mocking A Holiday Rock and Roll Party

That photographer I met at Doheny Blues hooked me up with a Malibu non-profit program to help orphaned children, called Safe Harbor Kids. I gladly gave enough to support two or three children at a special event. Later in the year, I got an invitation to attend a Christmas Party at East/West Recording Studio in LA. That evening Jackson Brown, one of my all-time favorite singer-songwriters, was there, along with his artist companion. The singer that recorded on Santana's Shaman Album with his own band, some of the original Chicago group and many others all gathered having been a part of the Malibu kid project, who knew? They jammed for us and played Christmas music too! What an absolute delight! I mocked that entire evening. Everything remains vivid in my recollection.

My photographer's friend was a greeter and she said she had to go out and do some coke, and asked if I would sit at the table and be a greeter for people. Well, ok, whatever, I thought that she meant a minute. However, she took her sweet time. Apparently, she did not just snort coke, she smoked some pot or something and drank some booze too. She came back pretty much toasted-wasted-in-the-bag-royally screwed up; thanking me profusely for watching the door, and telling me that she had I should hang out sometime. She said that she would love to have a threesome with me too! Oh boy, now that was appealing. Seriously, mocking the rock scene is the only way to go!! Rocking the Mock *"all day, all night Marianne."*

How to Mock a Wedding:

Mocking – it's the least you can do: It's the wedding of two people you adore, who wanted you to share in their big day and secretly are hoping you don't get stupid drunk and try to sleep with every groomsman all in the same night. They're just hoping and praying you'll maintain some of the cool, they totally appreciate about you.

People will be there from all over the country to celebrate the union of these two beautiful people. Your heart will sing when you soberly rock the mock at your friends' wedding, the most special day in their lives. The look of love undeniable, it will make you happy to actually see it and feel it. You might also get a bit jealous that it is not you with that perfect man.

Forget about jealousy on this special occasion, let your love light shine and maybe some single person will actually notice. Hey, come on, this day is not about you so try to keep this mock on track.

Truthfully, it is not that difficult to mock at a wedding. All the focus is on the bride and groom, as well it should be. The crowd also gets a big kick out of watching the blitzed wedding party attendants do the wildest things.

Yes, you can get in the Conga line, totally sober, you can do the Macarena without booze too! You can get just as happy and silly dancing and dipping without tipping over on the dance floor and the excellent news is you will have complete recollection of everything for years to come. This is true, no kidding, no blackouts, no pass outs, no crazy outrageous stories about you this time such a treat for everyone, you and the newlyweds.

You remember so much more of what actually happens when you're 100% on a mock. You're in your right heart and are you're in your right mind. There's not a single second of the most amazing event of your friends' big event lost – no hideous embarrassing episodes of you running naked in the woods, falling down drunk on the dance floor, or barfing in the women's toilet while the minister's wife holds your hair up out of the toilet bowl or helps you wipe the barf off the front of your silk dress.

You wake refreshed, thankful you don't have a splitting headache. You can actually go out to breakfast like a real person instead of trying to crawl out of bed looking for a bottle of painkiller or a little 'hair of the dog.'

Experiencing the wedding in all its glory completely 100%, alcohol-free is a fabulous experience and I highly recommend it. So do the newlyweds, and their families, trust me.

Mock Tale

Bev and I both attended Cynthia and John's wedding. Bev and Cynthia are so awesome! I would not mind being either of them when I grow up. Cynthia is the one who introduced me to the book *Calling in The One*. She like the rest of the women in her family who I am lucky enough to call my friends are all drop-dead gorgeous blue-eyed blondes. Cyn had men beating down her door but liked that book because it kept her from dating unacceptable partners. She found 'The One,' her soulmate. I watched her blossom and in so doing, she is now one of my new idols.

The bride's mother, the Duchess, and I went shopping for her dress for the wedding and reception. Somehow, it came up in talking with Bev that we were both mocking. We didn't know if it would be appropriate to bring our own mocks [BYOM]. I thought we might grab a bottle of fake bubbly and drag it along, but that didn't seem right. Just about that time in came the Wedding Reception

Bubbly Bar card and right along with all the other hot champagnes listed was the *Jackson "mock" champagne.* Cynthia and John think of everything!

I also mocked my son's wedding! I did so because I expected I might be a bit emotional and cry about things if I had any alcohol in my system. Good thing I did that, as I was very emotional and cried happy tears throughout the event, with no booze in my body. I can't fathom how much of a dither I'd have been in had I drank! It was a kick watching everyone partying at the reception – that Chris is quite the tap dancer!

I'll always remember with clarity, the nuance, and the personal attention the bride and groom paid to every detail. They touched so many lives with their love; it was a very joyful heartfelt experience for me. Hey, they now have a mother-son dance at the reception as well as the dad-and-daughter dance! Emily chose *Going to Carolina* for her dance, as her family is from Charlotte and my son picked *In My Life,* by the Beatles. We danced, we laughed, and I cried.

How to Mock Your Class Reunion

Good God in heaven, how long has it been since you got totally blitzed and fell down the hill three times that night saying goodbye to high school. Mocking the class reunion will not be as terrible as you imagine.

Sure, some if not all of your classmates will remember you as that fun party girl who was stoned and blitzed, shitfaced at most of the school functions, games and even at school on occasion. Well, those days are gone. You are now the Mock Star arriving on the scene to be the life of the party.

Only your flawless makeup, and dazzling smile will look just like that when you take your last dance around the dance floor with all the men who swear to God that they had a crush on you back in the day. Yes, they all say that: It's a guy thing. You smile and say I know you did, but you were Katie's guy, remember?

You will laugh at the outrageous things you once did, just get the biggest kick out of all those stories your old friends will be telling, of course, they were all part of the story! You might even tell some yourself! Then ask anyone to dance right then, because OMG, they are playing your favorite song!

Tip: Corner the bartender immediately to fix your drinks exactly the way you want them! You also need to tip him well, you do not want to hear, "*sorry honey we don't serve soft drinks in our alcohol glasses that is a rule.*"

I would go with the Cosmopolitan if possible. If they are using plastic solo cups, fine and dandy, drink any type concoction that suits you, no one will know or care. Time and so many things have a way of doing the hokey pokey and turning a life around.

Some of your classmates who never got blitzed, wasted, or stoned in high school may very well be on the road to life as an alcoholic now. A little love for old friends goes a long way. Hug them and let them know you adore them. Everyone loves being adored, respected, and loved, so do your best to lead with your heart and the rest will follow.

Have a grand time, dance even if you dance alone, make the rounds and talk with everyone, meet their spouse, or their partner. Wear your smile and let your old friends know how great it was to see them all one last time. Try it, I can tell you from experience it feels good.

I actually love my old classmates, and I told them so over a microphone, and I meant it.

It was a real heartfelt blast from the past!

	judgment, often good feelings, Less alertness, inhibition	steer vehicle, and react to emergency driving situations.
.08% About 4 alcoholic drinks**	Muscle coordination becomes poor (e.g., balance, speech, vision, reaction time, and hearing) Harder to detect danger Judgment, self-control, reasoning, and memory are impaired	Concentration Short-term memory loss Reduced speed control Reduced information processing capability (e.g., signal detection, visual search) Impaired perception
.10% About 5 alcoholic drinks**	Clear deterioration of reaction time and control Slurred speech, poor coordination, and slowed thinking	Reduced ability to maintain lane position and brake appropriately
.15% About 7 alcoholic	Far less muscle control than	Substantial impairment in vehicle control,

drinks**	normal	attention to driving task, and in necessary visual and auditory information processing
	Vomiting may occur (unless this level is reached slowly or a person has developed a tolerance for alcohol)	
	Major loss of balance	

*Blood Alcohol Concentration Measurement

The number of drinks listed represents the approximate amount of alcohol that a 160-pound man would need to drink in one hour to reach the listed BAC in each category. How much do you weigh? How many drinks do you consume in one hour?

**A Standard Drink Size in the United States

A standard drink is equal to 14.0 grams (0.6 ounces) of pure alcohol. Generally, this amount of pure alcohol is found in:

- 12-ounces of beer (5% alcohol content)
- 8-ounces of malt liquor (7% alcohol content)
- 5-ounces of wine (12% alcohol content)
- 1.5-ounces or a "shot" of 80-proof (40% alcohol content) distilled spirits or liquor (e.g., gin, rum, vodka, whiskey)

Source: Department of Transportation (US), National Highway Traffic Safety Administration (NHTSA). Traffic Safety Facts 2014 data: alcohol-impaired driving. Washington, DC: NHTSA; 2015 [cited 2016 Feb 5]

The many reports about women related fatal automobile accidents in the USA reveal a staggering number of these fatalities many times involve passengers, who are often children under the age of 14. Onsite blogs and social media groups celebrating moms liberated drinking is a social indicator that these behaviors are indeed becoming more prevalent than in past decades. Yet no one seems to have a real handle on why more women are driving drunk these days.

However, I doubt it takes a social science study to identify some likely contributing factors, indeed, some of the potential indicators revealed in *Party Like a Mock Star* may shine a little light on some of the possibilities. Notice that in our charts, women's weight factor alone, contributes to a higher degree of probability that they will get intoxicated easier.

I am not attempting to push our nations' social, party scene, into the prohibition era, or discourage the consumption of alcohol in every way! I am trying to impart using your best judgment. I am definitely not against anyone drinking booze. What I am trying to get across in this guide, is for women to recognize that the media hype in magazines, online, on billboards and in many shows and movies glamorizing the woman who can slam drinks down with the guys is aimed at selling alcohol. Nothing more and nothing less and all are the hype designed to affecting your lifestyle choices.

Party Like a Mock Star is here to give you some useful tools to avoid the alcohol traps, and how to drink the

Mocktail when it makes sense. Drinking alcohol in a safe and responsible manner is critical to self and others in so many ways. Aside, from the appearance and dating factors, which we spent, plenty of time on in this guide, the safety and health factors, not just yours, should be a significant consideration in when and how to consume alcohol.

An article, by Michelle Miller, an award-winning CBS News correspondent based in New York, reports that the number of women driving under the influence [DUI] arrests and fatalities have increased about 30% in the past decade.

While men still outnumber women by four to one in DUI arrests, drunken women fatal automobile crashes are more likely than men related fatal auto accidents, to have a child under the age of 14, in the car.

"Roughly 2,000 fatalities a year involve an impaired woman driver. This is clearly a very disturbing trend," said Ray LaHood, Secretary of Transportation. It is a trend, but it is definitely not as *trendy* as the alcohol drinking hype machine would lead you to believe as evidenced by these reports.

Join the Mocktail trend, which is the start of something new, and control the hype, maybe even change the hype! *That would be like driving a two-thousand-ton machine, the media.* As a matter of import, I have absolutely no idea how much media would weigh if media could be weighed, in pounds I mean. No, not the British pound, let's not get confused here.

It's not easy to lighten the truth about the trends and the potentially devastating effects of drinking and driving, that is not my intention. Drink responsibly and/or drink Mocktails when it makes sense! Let's go!

NEW YORK, NEW YORK!

Let us get this party started with New York City [NYC] New York, the city that never sleeps, where everything including Mocktails is the top of the top. I started my career in NYC on Park Avenue, Midtown Manhattan. I was so thrilled with the entire gig, there is no place like New York, and if you have not visited, you are missing the heartbeat of the country. I had it all and took a little bite out of the Big Apple. NYC is the most exciting city I have ever known. Loved her then, and love to visit her now!

Angel's Share, 8 Stuyvesant Street, 212-777-5415

The Mocktail: The Stella by Starlight

Yummy for your tummy, green apple, and shiso sorbet fill the bottom of a tall Champagne coupe with grassy, tart and sweet flavors topped off with ginger ale. The garnish is lemon with a special twist. Angel's Share is one of the first 'speak-easy' spots in NYC. This place has been a very popular secret in NYC for about 22 years.

The angel's share is more than just a great name for a club. Do you ever wonder how things and places got their names? I do, apparently. During the process of making wine or whiskey, producers use oak barrels to store their products. In storing the alcohol for long periods at an absolute temperature, some of the alcohol evaporates and the evaporating alcohol is the angel's share, going rightfully so to the guardian angels that watch over the liquor as it ages.

How to get in: Climb the stairs to the Japanese restaurant Village Yokocho, and enter through the unmarked wooden door in the back left. *Already it's a trip.* The Mocktail selection at this second-floor speakeasy is delicious we hear!

145

Shhhhhhhh: Angel's Share has another club aka the Annex, which reportedly has a shorter wait, and is just a walk from the original club. It is upstairs from Sharaku, at 14 Stuyvesant Street. The bar offers a view of the East Village and has a similar vibe to Angel's Share #1, is less crowded, has a slower pace and favored by a slightly more mature crowd according to online reviewers.

Clover Club, 210 Smith Street, Brooklyn, 718-855-7939

The Mocktail: The English Breeze

The easy breezy Mocktail is grapefruit tart mixed with sweet elderflower cordial blended together in the English Breeze, the result a Mocktail to whet your whistle! We hear that the mixologists are some of the best in the biz. We all need a little cheer and little of their English Breeze.

The NoMad, 1170 Broadway, 347-472-5660

The NoMad Hotel is located on the corner of 28th and Broadway. The NoMad is located in a great part of the City and easy to get to by any means of transportation. So, if you are a NoMad roaming from place to place, head on over to the NoMad where you will find a place to hang your hat. Every year The NoMad hosts their fabulous annual Masquerade Ball, a black tie, masks required New Year's Eve affair. Tickets for the event go fast, get them early in the year if you plan to attend.

Now for the drinking part, The NoMad has labeled their Mocktails *Soft Cocktails* yet there is an edge to them, so Soft Cocktail or Mocktail, here's the buzz.

THE MOCKTAIL: Paradise City

A fabulous concoction of no booze, just the schmooze: Grapefruit, passion fruit, vanilla, cream, topped with sparkling mineral water.

THE MOCKTAIL: Gingered-Ale

This Mock Star loves almost any Mocktail made with Ginger and sparkling mineral water, here is how the mixologist serves it at The NoMad: Ginger, lime, demerara sugar, topped with sparkling mineral water.

THE MOCKTAIL: Polka Man

I have a friend who loves polka dots! This one is for him: Pineapple, grapefruit, cold brew coffee, vanilla, strawberry, and lemon. Yeah man!

THE MOCKTAIL: Peter Piper

Pineapple, black pepper, pickled passion fruit, and lime; wonder if his wife likes this one?

THE MOCKTAIL: Tomato Soda:

Oh yes, this one sounds the best to this Mock Star! (although I would like to rename it to give it a Bloody Mary spin). Yet those names abound, and it's the taste and the visual we seek in our Mocktail!

They use tomato water, lemon verbena, celery, horseradish, in this concoction. I made it at home. I think the horseradish was the kicker!

The Wild Son, 53 Little West 12th St, New York, NY 10014

THE MOCKTAIL: (A variety of wild Mocktails)

Wild Son offers a long menu of non-alcoholic beverages e.g. Mocktails. They concoct their drinks with sodas, and juices made on-site with a carbonating system. They also serve nitro cold brew coffee, and an iced coconut milk latte offered on tap. How wild is that?

Riverpark, 450 East 29th Street, 212-729-9790

Located on an exclusive garden plaza, with views of the romantic East River, Riverpark is a destination spot in Manhattan's, Kip's Bay neighborhood.   Riverpark has several Mocktails on the bar menu, which you can find online. They call their Mocktails, Temperance Coolers and right now, they tell us each cost $6.

THE MOCKTAIL - The Butler

Apple Cider, Beet, Lemon, Cinnamon Syrup; ring me up one of these, please.

THE MOCKTAIL - Mr. Green

Cucumber, Lemon, Mint – simply clean, delish.

Riverpark grows its own produce on premises and that inspires what goes into the Mocktail Temperance Coolers. I tried this at home, with my own fresh ingredients and I liked it, Mr. Green.

The John Dory Oyster Bar, 1196 Broadway, 212-792-9000

THE MOCKTAIL: The Ginger Remedy:

Served up to mock the Hot Toddy drink, it is a honey-potent mug of ginger, lemon, and star anise and garnished with a cinnamon stick swizzle.

The Ginger Remedy is fashioned after the infamous Hot Toddy, used to quell anything that was ailing you. They made the real hot toddy with honey, whiskey and a twist of lemon at my house. My mom was a big fan of giving us youngsters a hot toddy for the body, usually a sore throat, and thanks again mom.

I'm infatuated with the name of the place; just love it! **The John Dory** also got a mention as one of the best Mocktails and 'pick-up' places in NYC. Looking for '*The One*' and a Mocktail, *The John Dory* may have all you seek.

The Stanton Social, 99 Stanton Street, 212-995-0099

THE MOCKTAIL: The Social Tea

Mocktail served in a sexy sophisticated snifter of gunpowder green tea and citrus with a taste of orange honey marmalade hits the spot; this is a hot drink. You will look good drinking it. The Stanton Social is one of the coolest Lower East Side lounges, with a slinky vibe and nod in décor to the nearby garment district. It's renowned, for its small plates, but word is their Mocktails are some of the best around. The three-story restaurant lounge is reminiscent of the luxe style and deco glamor of the 1940s. I love everything deco, thank you very much!

Gramercy Tavern, 42 East 20th Street, 212-477-0777

THE MOCKTAIL: The Cosmonot

A shaken no-booze-martini-made of a pinot noir type grape juice-grenadine topped with a citrus garnish. It looks as good as it tastes. The Gramercy is an unpretentious classic, it has gone through various iterations over the years and the latest reviews are fabulous, the New York Times gives it a three-star review.

Center Bar, 10 Columbus Circle, Fourth Floor, 212-823-9482

Shop until you drop then drop into Center Bar and center yourself. The drinks menu divided by notable booze eras, and includes the "Prohibition" era where you will find your Mocktails! They do not have their Mocktail menu online but your Mock Star sleuthed it out for you:

THE MOCKTAIL: The French Vanilla Soda

You sip of the French vanilla soda, in the Collins glass which gives it the Mocktail illusion, it's jazzed up with carbonated Chamomile-steeped simple syrup and vanilla extract, it is like a low-calorie root beer float only sexier. Don't you want one right now!

Atera, 77 Worth St, New York, NY 10013

Atera is a Basque word that translates to "To go out."

A recent article lets Mocktail lovers know that Atera masters the art of the non-alcoholic drink pairing, staking claim that it is, indeed, the city's best tasting menu pairing without a drop of alcohol.

The service captain at Atera starts by pouring from a chilled bottle of bubbly into a Riedel flute. OMG, be still my heart, love the bubbly and love the flute. The experts tell us that 'the liquid is brilliantly effervescent, vaguely sweet, and unusually piney – served with golden osetra caviar set atop pistachio ice cream."

THE MOCKTAIL: Champine

The place you can get your bubbly effervescent Champine is at Atera where it made and bottled. Champine is Artera's first pour of the restaurant's "temperance pairing" a name they like to call the Mocktail, darling, and that is cool with us! It's a six-drink progression, which diners order if, for whatever reason, they don't want to drink alcohol. Next trip to NYC, our Mock Stars are going in for the full experience. I want a case shipped to me for my next party!

WD-50

MOCKTAIL: Virgin Green Hornet

Tona Palomino former bar manager at WD-50 gives us the how-to-DYI juice on the Hornet and I added a few comments on the simple syrup part:

Finely chop four or five stalks of celery, puree in a blender, and strain through a sieve.

3 oz. celery juice

1/2 oz. lime juice

1/2 oz. simple syrup; see recipe below or you can also buy simple syrup pre-bottled.

Pour celery juice, lime juice, and simple syrup into an ice-filled shaker. Shake. Strain into a wine glass. Top with tonic water.

Simple syrup: Combine equal parts sugar and water in a saucepan. Bring to boil over medium heat; simmer until sugar dissolves. Cool. Buying the simple syrup pre-made saves a lot of time and effort. While it is not as authentic, it is easier to make at home. *Your call and not your last call by any means.*

LOS ANGELES

The City of Angels, Los Angeles has everything, and almost everything is glamorous including the Mocktail scene. In the past, I did my share of sipping, tasting imbibing in some of the best cocktails on the planet, cavorting in some of the finest places in the country. Yet cocktails are becoming so last year for some of us. Is that because Kim Kardashian does not drink alcohol? Well now, you know! Here we go with a few places and

Mocktails found in the city I love, to work, play and live these days!

Bacari P.D.R., 6805 S Vista Del Mar Lane, Playa Del Ray, CA 90293 (310-439-2100) www.bacaripdr.com

This classic California Casual is a few miles drive from LA proper, but you will love the off-the-wall-on-the-wall menu displayed on the floor to ceiling chalkboard. The beachside bar with an outdoor patio is the perfect place to unwind. You still dig a little Marvin Gaye and James Brown music, well hell yeah! The Bacari will serve that up for you too. Seriously have to get back there soon!!

THE MOCKTAIL: Cinnabark Swizzle ($5)

Tiki time, the Cinnabark, is a take on the 1950s tiki cocktail, no rum!

The mixologist mixes equal parts pineapple, grapefruit and cranberry juice with cinnamon syrup and a splash of club soda. This tiki-style drink served in a Collins glass with crushed ice, rocks. They add another cinnamon stick and a sprig of fresh mint. We want a tiny umbrella in ours too! We want a little more sizzle with our swizzle.

Gracias Madre, 8905 Melrose Ave, West Hollywood [WeHo], CA 90069 (323-978-2170)

www.graciasmadreweho.com

This is a fabulous upscale vegan, local, organic offshoot of Café Gratitude another beautiful place to eat and drink Mocktails. My gal-pal Robin and crew just hosted a birthday party at Gracias Madre, the perfect place for vegans and anyone who simply enjoys a relaxed vibe. Let's face it WeHo is a happening place any time of day or night. Just walking down the street in WeHo makes you deliriously happy, with zero-proof happy in your system.

Seriously, WeHo is one of my favorite places on the planet! The Gracias Madre creates a welcoming atmosphere; the setting is quite idyllic, with both indoor and outdoor seating. Opt for the outdoor seating it is quite romantic!

MOCKTAIL: A Shrubby for My Bubby II

House-made seasonal shrub- sea salt and co2

Ink., 8360 Melrose Ave., Ste. 107, Los Angeles, CA 90069 (323-651-5866) www.mvink.com

Ink, a fine dining experience, even the drinks go upscale. There are house-made sodas and a full menu of non-alcoholic drinks they think of everything.

Check out these yummy sounding Mocktail fashioned drinks served at the time of this writing:

- Cucumber mint, simple syrup, lime, club soda ($7)
- Strawberry green tea, yuzu, lemon, tonic ($7)
- Rosemary grapefruit, lime, tonic ($7)
- Carrot jasmine, ginger, lemon, club soda ($7)
- Sodas: Mexican coke, diet coke, sprite, fever tree ginger beer ($4)
- Art of tea: white tip jasmine, silver needle, Sencha, Egyptian chamomile, fresh mint, classic black, monk's blend ($5)

THE MOCKTAIL: Moscow Mule ($7)

We have heard they make a mean Moscow Mule too. It is just like the real deal but they replace the vodka with green tea and add mint for *kicks!*

Love & Salt

We love Vincenzo Marianella's vision and his mission to create Mocktails that satisfy and arouse the adult palate. Love & Salt goes with everything darling.

THE MOCKTAIL: Off the Funking Chain ($8)

It is so good you will be off the "funking chain": jalapeño, grapefruit juice, passion fruit, lime, ginger beer and honey syrup — topped with a grapefruit peel and jalapeño slice in a julep cup. Funk us up baby!

PUMP, 8948 Santa Monica Blvd., West Hollywood, CA 90069 (310-657-pump) www.pumprestaurant.com

Hanging out at PUMP is always a treat. It is exactly like visiting a magical garden. PUMP is just as sexy and exquisite, as its celebrity owner, Lisa Vanderpump. The entire wait staff is model perfect of course, enhancing the magical garden appeal. I happened to be there with Bev and we did not spot any Mocktails on the menu, but we were not worried. When I asked for my Mock Cosmo, the darling sexy waiter asked, *"So, sweetie would you like a Mocktail?"* Well, hello that is what we need! Bev had one too. The Mocktail had the perfect taste, look, and image, without the booze. I had two and was driving!

THE MOCKTAIL: Mock Cosmopolitan

Custom made to my particular taste, just like ordering a real cocktail, the waiter let me tell him exactly how I wanted it and that is exactly how I got it! Cranberry juice, sprite®, a twist of lime, sugar on the edge of the sexy martini glass with a slice of lemon sitting pretty on the rim, perfection.

Villa Blanca, 9201 Brighton Way, Beverly Hills, CA 90210 (310-859-7600) www.villablancarestaurants.com

After the PUMP experience, we took our Mocktail crawl to another Vanderpump restaurant, the Villa Blanca, in Beverly Hills. As one might imagine, Villa Blanca has an understated sex appeal, as the designer Lisa Vanderpump, envisioned, it is luxe, sultry and sublime. We opted for seating just inside the open doors leading to the outdoor seating, the best of both. We enjoyed the fabulous atmosphere, stayed as long as time would allow and could actually drive afterward! We dreamed up our own clean tasting refreshing elegant looking Mocktail. Here you go!

MOCKTAIL: Seltzer with a Lime Twist

BOA, 9200 Sunset Blvd., West Hollywood, CA 90069

The BOA Steakhouse is my go to place in WeHo. The atmosphere, the garden space, the lounge, and dining room are all gorgeous. The wait staff is equally beautiful and treats you like the VIP Mock Star you are when you arrive and in every step of the experience. The food is fabulous, you must try their Cesar Salad while there, and watching them make it tableside is a special treat. Wait, let's get back to the Mocktails, you ask for it; you got it.

I often opt for the Mock Cosmopolitan because I just love the martini glass at my table. I think we have established that from the frequent reference made to it here.

Get ready for a treat, Tara Shadiz, who we feature in this little *Party like a Mock Star!* will be making some of her own fabulous Mocktail creations for us in person, at the BOA, for our *Party Like a Mock Star* video episodes!

MOCKTAIL: Mock Cosmopolitan

Cranberry – sprite – twist of lime and a very secret ingredient that my mixologist didn't disclose, served in a sexy martini glass!

155

Magnolia House, 492 S Lake Ave, Pasadena, CA (626-584-1126) www.themaghouse.com

Yes, this is a bit outside the Los Angeles, but just a tad. We wanted to include this one because of its rich history and the cool neighborhood. The latest iteration of this Pasadena craftsman-house-turned-liquor store the Magnolia House is now a finely tuned bar. Beverage guru Evan Zimmerman creates swanky Mocktails as an interesting addition to his swanky drink menu. Everybody gets happy!

THE MOCKTAIL: Cherry and Lime Rickey ($6)

This cherry is all killer no alcohol filler.

Start with fresh-pressed cherry juice, layer with lime juice and honey; a non-alcoholic drink with the complexity of its lime rickey booze filled counterpart. Let's toast to that!

CHICAGO

Chicago is truly the windy city and you can really get 'blown away' there. We got 'blown away' there a time or two, primarily in the Blues or Jazz clubs, which stay open until 4 am and 5 am. Even with a pre-power-nap, I could never stay up that late! That is right, when you want to get your music and dance vibe on or just be out past your regular bedtime Chicago is your City. Chicago really does have what you would call a bar scene; that is in addition to the club scene. There is a definite distinction and the only bar I would ever actually want to enter are those with the blues or jazz music being the primary focus like those in Chicago. *When the focus is on music and dance, it takes the focus off from alcohol.* While some clubs have rules about a two-drink minimum, you can make friends by buying alcohol for someone else's table. You can also order a virgin concoction of the alcoholic counterpart. You might not be as popular with the bartender or server ordering a Mocktail, but tip them well and they will get over it soon enough. Chicago is a big city with a cool laid-back vibe.

The blues is a Chicago thing, yet the jazz history in Chicago is equally a Chicago thing. Both grew up about the same time. While the blues stays pretty faithful to the roots, jazz rambles around a bit; just like you will be doing when you are out and about in Chicago; rambling around a bit. If you are in Chicago and you are into music to go with your Mocktail, you can try these places and dance your brains out to some great live music. Don't worry about libations – any of these spots can hook you up with a Mocktail. Some have little dance floors and some are huge, but even those without any dedicated dance floor will let you get your woogie on girl! Yes, I *do* know this from experience. You need to show proof that you are 21 or over to get into many of the places mentioned next, even if you are only going in for your dance and to rock your Mock.

The Underground Wonder Bar, 10 E Walton St, Chicago, IL 60611-1413 (Gold Coast) (312-266-7459)

Expect to pay a cover charge, which you will not regret, live music, jazz, blues, funk, and even an open mic night. Dress code is simple. Do not show up naked! They have a big dance floor. You can blend right in to dance and have fun without the booze. Remember if there is a drink minimum, buy them, give them away, and make new friends.

Andy's Jazz Club, 11 E Hubbard St, Chicago, IL 60611 (312-642-6805)

Steeped in a rich history, Andy's is one of the best known and respected Jazz Clubs in Chicago but is also home to Traditional, Swing, Bop, Fusion, Latin, and Afro-Pop, they do it all and they do it well at Andy's. They allow partygoers under age 21 in for the 7 pm and 9 pm shows with a dinner reservation. Take in the early shows and drink non-alcoholic drinks with the underage. Once the 9:45 pm show starts everyone under 21 is on their way out the door. The Club closes its doors at 1 am.

The Berkshire Room, ACME Hotel entrance 15 East Ohio Street, Chicago, IL 60611

The Berkshire Room is a class act Craft Cocktail Lounge, the kind that stories have been written. Indeed, plenty of articles have appeared in publications from The Chicago Tribune to Esquire Magazine, the Berkshire is a recipient of numerous cocktail awards. While they do not have Mocktails listed on their menu, try the Dealer's Choice option. Big help to know your stemware and your taste profile, when ordering your Dealer's Choice. In other words, have a clue what you like when your order. Just tell the fabulous mixologist, who will then make a Mocktail to your specification. Your bartender will explain what is shaken, stirred, blended or mixed into your Mocktail. The Berkshire Room closes at 3 am on Saturday nights.

THE MOCKTAIL: Dealer's Choice

This one is a wildcard and we're leaving it up to you!

Three Dots and a Dash, 435 N Clark, Chicago, ILL (312-610-4220) www.threedotschicago.com

Three Dots is an authentic tiki-themed hotspot that everyone is raving about all over the city, online, on Yelp, and it's all good. Like most clubs in Chicago, it stays open late but not as late as some; Three Dots closes at 3 am. While they do not actually list any nonalcoholic options on the drink menu, the mixologists are up for mixing you a Mocktail from any of their alcoholic originals. Tiki drinks were born to morph into delicious Mocktails.

THE MOCKTAIL: The Bunny's Banana Daiquiri

This drink is what you might imagine. It is a frozen blend of coconut, banana, lime, and nutmeg. Big surprise, it's topped off with a banana-dolphin garnish. Great glass and fabulous garnish, I would order it just for that banana-dolphin! We are not even going to ask why it's called the Bunny's delight.

Allium Bar in the Four Seasons Hotel, 120 East Delaware Place Chicago (312-808-1100)

I love staying at this hotel and have frequented the Allium on each occasion. Aside from the fantastic cuisine, the views are breathtaking. The Four Seasons is located near Lake Michigan, the Magnificent Mile and North Michigan Avenue where you can shop until you drop. After you fall, pick yourself back up, with one of the Allium Mocktails.

THE MOCKTAIL: Strawberry Mint Lemonade

The name says it all; it is a refreshing summer drink and it is not summer all year in Chicago! So get this one while it's hot!

THE MOCKTAIL: Ginger Fizz ($8)

An Apple cider, pomegranate, and ginger beer concoction for cooler weather. Go for it and sit by the fireside.

SAN FRANCISCO

San Francisco my 'City by the Bay' was my home for over twenty years I have met *'some loving people there'*. I did not live until I lived in "The Emerald City." Though times have changed it a little, it remains one of the most romantic cities in the USA. I still own my little cottage in the hills and visit there regularly, as I definitely left a part of my heart in San Francisco, just like everyone else. I got pretty smashed, lit, looped, and sloshed in The City back in the day, but I have since discovered the San Francisco Mocktail scene. This foodie city is serving incredibly good Mocktails too.

Burritt Room, 417 Stockton Street (between Bush and Sutter streets); (415-400-0555)

THE MOCKTAIL: Orange Flower Limeade ($6)

Chilled limeade contains a taste of orange flower-some olio sacrum spiced citrus oil made from pressing lime and lemon peels with sugar, clove, and nutmeg. Chew on the sage garnish after. It's a San Francisco treat!

Bourbon and Branch, 501 Jones Street (at O'Farrell Street); (415-346-1735)

THE MOCKTAIL: Maple Basil Crunch ($5)

This is a ridiculously fantastic drink. The Maple Basil Crunch will blow your mind. Just imagine; basil being able to add the essential zip without the booze? Ladies strut into the Bourbon and Branch. Ask for one of their Maple sugar and spice with everything nice Mocktails.

El Techo Lolinda, 2518 Mission Street (at 21st Street); (415-550-6970)

THE MOCKTAIL: Virgin Piña Colada ($6)

How many virgin piña coladas can you drink? The creamy pineapple and coconut cream over crushed ice, topped with a sprinkle of cinnamon are seriously intoxicating, while leaving you 100% booze-free.

Hakkasan, 1 Keary Street (at Geary Street); (415-829-8148)

THE MOCKTAIL: Virgin Hakka ($8)

Hakkasan takes cocktails very seriously, complete with serving up its signature drink Mocktail style. The creamy, frothy coconut and lychee bevy paired with homemade, passion fruit syrup, is an excellent reason to stop by.

Ken Ken Ramen, 2278 18th Street (at Mission Street); (415-967-2336)

THE MOCKTAIL: Hot Zombie ($6)

Hot Zombie: Thai chili-infused lemonade mixed with açai and mango juice. How hot is that!

Millennium, 580 Geary Street (at Jones Street); (415-345-3900)

THE MOCKTAIL: *Raw-volution, $7*

Yum, kombucha, muddled apricot, mint, strawberry, and lime juice, for a citrus Mocktini. The drink is finished off with homemade ginger agave syrup and dehydrated citrus peels, then garnished with razor-thin slices of cucumber and strawberry. Are we there yet? Oh yeah, and the menu is kicking. I ate there a lot during my raw food phase.

Novela, 662 Mission Street (between New Montgomery and Annie Street Alley); (415-896-6500)

THE MOCKTAIL: Helen Keller ($6)

It's Mojito type concoction; the Helen Keller Mocktail is a sweet and tangy zero-booze tonic that mixes cranberry juice, pineapple syrup, and ginger beer, made complete with the mint garnish; it's nearly as good as the Zoejito and clearly you *will* be able to drive home after! Big hit!

Rich Table, 199 Gough Street (at Oak Street); 415-355-9085

THE MOCKTAIL: Grapefruit Signature Refresher ($5)

Located in Hayes Valley, Rich Table has three signature refreshers; the Grapefruit Elderflower-St. Germaine type citrus cooler; elderflower garnish will have you drunk with freshness in no time, zero-proof, and no hangover.

Slow Club, 3583 16th Street (at Noe); (415-252-7500)

THE MOCKTAIL: The Juno ($4.50)

Juno: the goddess of marriage and wife of Jupiter: You are going to fall in love with The Juno Mocktail made from muddled blackberries, fresh lemon, rosemary, basil and honey syrup, orange bitters, and seltzer. Enjoy a chill spot, with a good vibe – and check out Noe Street, with its European ambiance, it's heavenly.

Starbelly, 2501 Mariposa Street (at Hampshire Street); 415-241-9390.

THE MOCKTAIL: Darjeeling Cooler, $5

Darjeeling tea tea-inspired, mixed with lime and basil served up with a side of frothy, egg-white foam and a few drops of bitters on top. Found in the Castro, the Starbelly serves up Mocktails so sensational you would swear you were drinking a real cocktail, but you aren't!

BOSTON AIN'T ALL WICKED DUNKIES

It has been awhile since I have been around, around, and around Boston. Seriously, a police officer in Boston pulled me over to the curb of the circle one day saying he had seen me loop around a hundred times, he was exaggerating, slightly. He asked where I was going. We could both see the place from where he was standing.

"Why don't you just pull down that street right there," he pointed it out while he asked.

"Because," I answered, *"it says NO TURN."* I was nearly crying.

He then said as a matter of fact *"Oh don't pay any attention to the traffic signs here – no one does."*

So, if you are from out of town do yourself a favor, order a driver, you are going to find some great food, good folks and mouthwatering Mocktails. *Cheers!*

Alden & Harlow, 40 Brattle St., Cambridge, 617-864-2100, aldenharlow.com

THE MOCKTAIL: The Grapeful Dead

The mixologist concocts a mix of grapefruit juice with housemade ginger beer, smoked celery agave nectar, and fresh lime juice and we are 'Grapeful'. Cool name, cool drink.

Backbar, 7 Sanborn Ct., Somerville, 617-718-0249, backbarunion.com

THE MOCKTAIL: Tropical Heat Wave

An unusual combination of pineapple juice, cocoa nib tea, and chipotle/cinnamon syrup.

Especially when there is a bit of a nip in the air, tropical heat/health wave is just what the doctor ordered.

Bistro du Midi, 272 Boylston St., Boston, 617-426-7878 www. bistrodumidi.com.

THE MOCKTAIL: Verte

And green it is, muddled cucumber, green tea, and lime

A fabulous French restaurant with an exceptional wine list, Bistro du Midi's star sommelier Todd Lipman is bringing some incredible French flare to the Mocktail menu too!

Café ArtScience, 650 E. Kendall St., Cambridge, 857-999-2193, cafeartscience.com

THE MOCKTAIL: Mango and Rosemary

Ginger beer and lime, with a mango-and-rosemary-layered ice cube yum!

THE MOCKTAIL: Orange Creamsicle

A grown up Creamsicle to delight your adult palate, orange blossom water, condensed dairy, orange peel dust, and a clarified orange ice ball! I can't help but love this one!

THE MOCKTAIL: Zen Coolie

A concoction to calm your nerves, hibiscus iced tea, rose water, honey, and peppermint ice shards- this is a cool laid back drink.

The Frogmore, 365 Centre St., Jamaica Plain, 857-203-9462, thefrogmore.com

THE MOCKTAIL: Shifting Winds

Pomegranate, ginger, lemon, and soda it will blow your mind!

THE MOCKTAIL: Sweater Weather

Grapefruit and lime accented with cardamom are *hot*!

Island Creek Oyster Bar, 500 Commonwealth Ave., Boston, 617-532-5300, *islandcreekoysterbar.com*

THE MOCKTAIL: Abigail's Delight

A soda of fresh pineapple, with goodies mixed in and it is all house-made; such a delight.

THE MOCKTAIL: Lizzie Swizzle or sparkling Wags #2,

Pomegranate syrup and fresh lemon we think Lizzie has Swizzle!

Liquid Art House, 100 Arlington St., Boston

THE MOCKTAILS: Passionfruit Lemonade and Red Lychee drinks

Lolita, 271 Dartmouth St., Boston
617-369-5609, lolitatequilabars.com

THE MOCKTAIL: Vinedo

Mocktail wine, be still my wino's heart. My favorite:

Blended white and concord grapes, fresh berries, and orange, faux wine! Yes please, the Vinedo beckons!

THE MOCKTAIL: Mojitos Innocente

The whole mojitos vibe without the rum; order it by the glass or get a pitcher for the table. I love this one too.

These are two of my all-time favorites, just saying...

Mei Mei, 506 Park Dr., Boston
857-250-4959, meimeistreetkitchen.com

THE MOCKTAIL: Hot Buttered Fire Cider

Fiery- a mix of ginger, honey, chilies, and butter.

This creative restaurant got its start as a food truck, now folks enjoy the fare without the truck! Along with some excellent drinks without the booze, it's a win-win!

Sarma, 249 Pearl St. Somerville
617-764-4464 sarmarestaurant.com.

THE MOCKTAIL: Sumac Lemonade, Saffron Sharbat

A party in your mouth with coriander, soda with saffron, rose, and citrus *'I'm just mad about Saffron and...'*

THE MOCKTAIL: The Buzz Aldrin

Tang®, made with orange, cinnamon, and sage, check!

I just had to know why they named the drink the Buzz Aldrin. I get the Tang® part because we all know they took Tang® to the moon. Buzz Aldrin was the second human to walk on the Moon, but the first and perhaps the only to urinate in his space suit as his first act on the Moon, little-known fact unless you are following moonwalks, and I'm not talking *Michael Jackson* style here! NASA *suspects* Armstrong and he were sober at the time. Back on planet Earth, however, it is widely known that Buzz lived up to his nickname. The Buzz Aldrin Mocktail is a tangy treat that lacks the liquor but certainly not the adventure. Be sure to use the bathroom first, even if you think you do not have to go.

Shojo, 9A Tyler St., Boston, 617-423-7888

THE MOCKTAIL: Lavender Bitter Tonic,

This yummy Mocktail blends a mix of grapefruit, lavender and lemon flavors.

Are you into old kung-fu movies and hip-hop music? The Shojo has your mojo.

BEST MOCKTAILS IN MEMPHIS TENNESSEE

"Long distance information, give me Memphis Tennessee Help me find the party trying to get in touch with me" - Chuck Berry

The numbers you require are listed next:

Bari Ristorante, 22 Cooper St.; 901-722-2244

The Mocktail: The Bernie was styled by the bartender, Vincent Hale and named for politician Bernie Sanders and was mentioned earlier in this guide, but here it is again in case you missed it!

Shaken not stirred: To make, use fresh grapefruit juice; a splash of fresh lemon juice and Fever Tree ginger beer; add a touch of cherry juice and top it off fresh rosemary, and voila. Shake it up and pour it into a sexy fluted champagne glass topped with ginger beer.

It does not end there, and I know you are salivating; now squeeze the rind from the grapefruit over the drink and add a twist of grapefruit peel and a swig of rosemary for garnish. I want this drink now. Bring on The Bernie, I feel the Bern! How did they miss a chance to be voting on the Bernie in 2016? Not this drink, voters online all voted yes!

Felicia Suzanne's, 80 Monroe Ave.; 901-523-0877

THE MOCKTAIL: Virgin Strawberry Mule

It is made of mint, lime, muddled strawberries and ginger beer. Sounds like a kick without the after kick in the head.

Cafe Pontotoc, 314 South Main St.; 901-249-7955

Bartender Cady Smith mixes up some tasty Mocktails and folks are talking about it!

THE MOCKTAIL: Cady's Cooler

Crafted of mango, orange, pomegranate, cranberries with a splash of grenadine: Cady claims to add a dash of love and a little umbrella too. We love Cody too!

The Hard Rock Café, 126 Beale St.; 901-529-0007

Mocktail listings at the Hard Rock called, *"Alternative Rock"* which I think rocks the mock! I want the groupie grind, and I do not care what's in it, it just sounds perfect!

THE MOCKTAILS: Wildberry Smoothie, Mango Tango, Strawberry Basil Lemonade, Mango-Berry Cooler and my favorite: The Groupie Grind.

MOCKTAIL: The Groupie Grind

A concoction of mango purée, piña colada mix, and pineapple juice blended with a strawberry swirl and it is a groupie delight, right on, far out man!

NEW ORLEANS THE BIG EASY

Et toi! My great uncle used to play piano on Bourbon Street that is until he drank it dry. My nephew, an artist, and NOLA resident, enjoys of driving a handsome cab, with his little dog, Jack Daniels, by his side.

I volunteered to work the legendary Jazz and Heritage Festival in New Orleans [NOLA], the first such festival following the massive Hurricane Katrina. I wanted to give back, to the City, to the music I adore and to the festival itself. I worked backstage handing out the checks to the performers after their gig. That's right, it *is* your check *in hand*, not in the mail, best job at the Fest; everyone was looking for me!

NOLA, The Big Easy, Crescent City, the Birthplace of Jazz is a place no one on the planet should miss: It is another world. It is rich with diversity, the world's best music, some amazing hoofers, and excellent cuisine. Nothing about it is like anything place else in the country. I did my share of hitting the clubs, downing those sliders, and dancing until we shot out the lights in the French Quarter. It's a party place like no other! However, the Big Easy just got *easier* for those of us who are now into Mocktails vs Cocktails. Let the good times roll! *Laissez les bons temps rouler!*

There are so many bars in the French Quarter that you do not have to travel far to hit the next one, a pub-crawl it is easy. Finding great Mocktails while less prominent are out there and they mix them up with NOLA flare. My Crewe just did the pub-crawl on Halloween night in NOLA, the brave souls. The Pino's shared real-time reviews, as they did their first juice crawl! Love that kind of night, especially when you wake up the next day without the hangover from hells-Ville.

Most good bartenders can make you a great Mocktail. Nevertheless, we put our Mock Star Crewe in NOLA on a juice-pub-crawl, hitting the places people are talking about to try the Mocktails that people are raving about. Here is the Pino's take in NOLA Rocking the Mock!

The Pino's started at **Latitude 29** and tried a few Tiki themed Mocktails on for size. Jeff 'Beachbum' Berry, tiki expert and co-owner of Latitude 29, spent 30 years studying drink menus on several continents. Knowing his booze, he decided what his place needed was a few great nonalcoholic tiki drinks alongside the boozy originals; good plan! The entire place has a Tiki bar vibe, always a classic. The Pino's are discerning drinkers; are natives and know what is hot and what is not! They report that the Mocktails at Latitude 29 will not disappoint, they are delicious, *"Great tiki ambiance, with our famous NOLA courtyard atmosphere, the drinks were great! We thought the Mocktails might have been a bit on the higher price end at ($7) But the price was soon of absolutely no concern, as all of the ingredients were fresh squeezed, and excellent, **more** than worth the price".* They were so ready for some zing without the sting? They say you should try these Tiki Mocks:

THE MOCKTAIL: The Colada Con Nada, ($7)

They say the drink is based on the bar's Kea Colada, with a dash of passion fruit and without the rum. You will not even miss it.

Jeremy's take on the drink, *"The Colada Con Nada was very smooth going down. Tip: When you order, ask for less ice and more drink you will 'like it like it like that'!"*

THE MOCKTAIL: Re-Animator, ($7)

A Zombie Mockail? Sacrilegious but delicious.

Becca, our Mocktail cutie in NOLA, tells us, *"The Re-Animator is a very snappy drink. This zombie goes down just like the real thing, and it is not as sweet as you might imagine. I'll have another."*

THE MOCKTAIL: Missionary's Fallback ($7)

This concoction is based on the Missionary's Downfall, minus the downfall.

Next stop, the Kingfish. W*e are walking down to the Kingfish now,* as we get the real time play by play, *'Wow, the Kingfish is slammed tonight"* yet, our crewe got seats at the bar, where the Mocktails got rave reviews, from our newly recruited, Mock Stars, on location. *"Everything is house-made at the Kingfish and that got our attention right out of the gate!"* As they were slurping, taking in the wild Halloween partying, they were served some mighty fine Mocktails stating, *"these are awesome, we got the Vanilla cream soda; oh holy shit, the cream soda is like drinking a vanilla cloud."*

Kingfish, 337 Chartres St., *504.598.5005*

MOCKTAILS: The Whole Darn Menu

Mexican Coca-Cola ($3)

Made with real cane sugar

Tonic ($3)

House made-Tonique au Qinprine Sirup, charged water

Ginger Beer ($3)

House-made ginger syrup, house-made gum syrup, lemon juice, lime juice, and charged water

Celery Soda ($3)

Lime juice, house-made gum syrup, and bitter truth celery, bitters, and charged water

Angesture Soda ($4)

House-made pineapple syrup, lime juice, extinct add phosphate, charged water

Pineapple Soda ($4)

House-made pineapple syrup, lime juice, an acid phosphate, and charged water

Strawberry Soda ($4)
House-made strawberry syrup, lime juice, an extinct acid phosphate, and charged water
Vanilla Lactart Soda ($5)

House-made vanilla syrup, house-made gum syrup, cream lactart, and charged water

Strawberry Shake ($5)

House-made strawberry syrup, cream, whole egg, and charged water

Do not let the names of these Mocktails fool you, as alcohol-free as they sound, and as zero-proof as they truly are, served, *Big Easy* style, with a flare that dares to kick the tail off a real cocktail. They have you covered at the Kingfish.

Note: Designated drivers [DD] enjoy free Mocktails. DD must be sober and accompanied by a patron or patrons partaking of alcoholic beverages. So Mockers here is a place you can take your drinking party and your drinks are on the house. Rock that Mock in the Big Easy!

Bar Tonique, *820 N Rampart St.* (504-324-6045)

Our new Mocktail converts, in training, on location in NOLA, were into Bar Tonique, here is what they had to say, *"Very cool atmosphere. It is in an old world NOLA building with a modern twist, and what we considered a very tasteful NOLA, design. It is a great place, on Rampart Street, which has just been revived, by the addition of the streetcar line. Drinking or not it makes it easy to get around. With all house-made syrups, the Vanilla cream was smooth and delightful. We could not decide if it was like drinking a cloud or the best 'melted ice cream' we ever had! We were surprised at how much we loved these and will have them again."*

Jeremy adds, *"This ginger beer had the bite I was craving from a cocktail without the booze! We could have spent the rest of the night here."*

Diaz the brainchild at the Tonique shies away from the term, "Mocktails"; instead, he calls them "temperance drinks". He has a lengthy selection of nonalcoholic sodas and shakes on the menu and if he prefers the term Temperance drinks that is just fine with us.

"Hey, it was Halloween celebration night in NOLA! So going out and seeing all the crazy costumes and people falling down drunk, was a kick. We were glad to get dressed up and try new things, just what the doctor ordered for a couple of NOLA parents. We got all the

crazy without the hangover! Thanks, Z we both needed it, so glad you hooked us in on the fabulous, Mocktail scene. Wish we could have gone to a couple more places, but the Mocktail crawl could only go on just so long; especially, with the Halloween crowd out doing their thing! We will be back to Mock again!" The Pino Crewe

Thanks to the Pino's we got all the juice on the juice in NOLA! Love you guys!!

SALT LAKE CITY, UTAH

I did a gig in Salt Lake for the famous Harmon Kardon manufacturing facility, just on the outskirt of Salt Lake. This was one of the best projects I have been involved with for a few reasons; primarily watching those guitar men, testing the sound systems throughout the manufacturing plant. My proclivity for digging guitar players goes a long way back, yet I remained very professional.

Afterward, my associate and I went out for a wrap-up dinner meeting.

All around us, the restaurant diners had wine at their place settings. Despite that, we could not find a wine list to save our souls.

Finally, we asked our server who was sporting tasteful tats and wearing a few discrete piercings, how those people got wine. She said, *"Oh would you like to see a wine list?"* Well, yes we did. She told us it was against the rules to bring us a list of libations but were allowed to provide the list if asked. I could not help it. I had to know. *"Where do you and your friends go dancing and have a few cocktails?"* I asked.

She lowered her voice to tell us that there was a few "speak-easy" word of mouth places that people went to imbibe.

I understand the speakeasy is outdated and they are now out in the open. Yet, the restaurant law in the city of Salt Lake remains. Check it out: Having a drink, a beer or a glass of wine with dinner, no problem, but, your server must first ask whether you will be eating. Then, only *if* you ask about an alcoholic beverage will you be allowed to see the cocktail menu.

However, if you do not ask about food first, and have a cocktail before you read the menu; it is a violation of law.

Restaurant owners who violate the law may be fined or lose their license. The Utah liquor official's reports are downplaying this legislation and the enforcement of it because they are afraid of negative media it would attract, especially around ski season.

Ladies, I would not worry about it. Try a restaurant of your choice, relax, enjoy, have fun, experience a great meal and if you want you could definitely ask for a Mocktail. You got this ladies!

I decided to add Salt Lake City Mock tale, because of my earlier experience there, because of the people I know who ski there regularly and because I came upon an article about two extraordinary young women who created a business on the mantra, *"Schmooze without the Booze!"*

As stated earlier a great deal of my work involves attending functions and after work networking events so the schmooze factor in their story intrigued me, drew me in.

It seems that Ms. Ann Marie Wallace who has always been a non-drinker has lived by that mantra. She says that most 33-year-olds non-drinkers evidentially grow tired of soda and tonic. There's a news flash!

While on campus at Utah State, she and her business partner Jenna Glover threw quite a few parties for others on campus back in the day. Their mission was to create no-booze drinks that they found tasty.

As it turned out, the drinks were a big hit with the partygoers and soon college students on campus were asking them to create more parties. The word got around.

Both Wallace and Glover went into the workplace after university and found the same thing we all do in the business world, that most of the events they attend always involved alcohol. It is just part of doing "business."

They decided to take charge of their environment and help others out as well. They put their heads together and got back into the mixology game.

They created their own mobile bartending company called ConcoXions. That is right they took their show on the road.

They set up the bar with the requisite fancy stemware and garnish of course, and mix the drinks for the guests.

Wallace also wanted her creations to be more than an alcoholic drink minus the liquor, so they create drinks uniquely their own and come up with some funny creative names to jive the Utah conservative population just a touch.

Due to Salt Lake's history around the consumption of alcohol, I believe that ConcoXions mobile bartending service found their niche. As mentioned before life is full of so many reasons to celebrate and ConcoXions had the panache to create parties and celebrations that bring all the *"Schmooze without the Booze!"*

I have a decent Mocktail bar setup at my place and opt for the pre-mixed bottles of mixer simply because it is easy. I am pleased as punch that ConcoXions who shared some of their recipes online also use some pre-mixed ingredients.

I was slightly disappointed that I could not find their ConcoXion drink recipe called the *Polygamy Punch*, with the tagline *"You're gonna want more than one."* That drink must be a hoot at a party. I got busy and tried several of their other ConcoXions. If they are still on the road with this gig, we have to get them to Los Angeles!

Source: ConcoXions specialty drinks and bartending:

Point 00

Such a fun twist on the 0.08 blood-alcohol level it takes to get you a DUI citation in Utah. I mixed this one up in a moment and found that it actually had layers of flavor.

I particularly enjoyed the fact that I did not have to try to make my own sweet and sour mix, thank you very much.

I also enjoyed how this drink looked in my very special rock glass.

When you mix up a drink like this one, pour it into your unique glass and love it you know you will be mixing these up for your guests. Here's the recipe:

Point 00

Ice
3 ounces lemonade
3 ounces pineapple juice
Splash of sweet and sour mix
Splash of grenadine
Lemon wedge, for garnish
Stemware:
10-ounce rocks glass

Fill a 10-ounce rocks glass half full with ice. Add lemonade, pineapple juice, sweet and sour mix and grenadine. Garnish with a lemon wedge. Love that they use pre-mixed things for those times you are just in a rush.

Source: ConcoXions specialty drinks and bartending:

ConcoXions came up with a Virgin Bubbly that I think is even better than the one I came up with and mine is not bad. It is not that easy to get a great Bubbly without the champagne. Nevertheless, I enjoyed their recipe. The ginger ale gives it the bubbly effect you need in a bubbly and I think the raspberries for garnish added a yummy touch. My family and guests will get a taste of this on our retreat.

MOCKTAIL: Virgin Bubbly

1-ounce white grape juice
1-ounce ginger ale
1-ounce apple juice
3 fresh raspberries, for garnish (it isn't always easy to get fresh raspberries so I think I will experiment with strawberries on my next batch).
Stemware: 5-ounce fabulous champagne flute

MOCKTAILS IN AUSTIN TEXAS

One of the most popular online dating sites on the planet, dug through the billions of their online dating profiles to see if they could identify the booziest cities in the USA.

It is always good to know that whatever you put on your online profile is honest to the point of creating a study around it. Better yet, that any of your information, can be 'mined', for whatever purpose, at any time.

The report I read had no names attached, at least. With that stated, to qualify as one of the booziest cities in the USA, an individual had to check the box **'REGULARLY'** drinks alcohol on their dossier, for the entire world to see. Either daters in Austin or more honest than the rest of the country or they simply drink more as this study suggests.

I was surprised that Austin came in number one on this game show and New Orleans took a third place ribbon this year. Not to knock NO, I love that place. I also enjoy Austin Texas. I think Austin has a revitalization going on that is bringing in more music, more art and has a lot going on in the culinary arts as well.

Yes, I do recall quite a lot of drinking there too. Yet, the organic, vegan, homemade foods and beverages were one of the big selling points for me when staying in Austin. That is why I was surprised to learn that they ranked number one booziest city, not sure if we should send a note of congrats on that one.

I did run across an article that claims the hottest club trend happening in Austin this year, does not contain a single drop of booze in it, nada, zip, zero-booze. This article claimed that Mocktails are the new deal in Austin town after sundown. One and one are not adding up to two with these conflicting stories.

Yet, there are always two sides to everything and co-owner of the craft cocktail haven Drink says they are serving up more and more Mocktails than ever before.

The bartender should know, bartenders really do know what people are drinking. People are just demanding drinks that are more non-alcoholic these days.

It's Mocktail time in Austin. I believe that Austin may very well be on the cutting edge of the Mocktail scene!

All the better reason for a Mock Star to visit there again, real soon!

Here are just a couple of places to check out:

Opal Devine's Austin Grill, 12709 North Mopac Expressway, Austin, TX 78727 (512-733-5353)

We hear you can get a get a mighty fine Mocktail at Opal Devine's but they do not have the Mocktails listed; so we will just have to believe what we heard on the vine. This place is a vegetarian and organic foodie's delight. They make most of their ingredients fresh for the crafted cocktails. We bet they can mix you up a big ole juicy Mocktail.

Bar Congress, 200 Congress Ave, Austin, Texas 78701 (512-827-2760)

The Bar Congress is repeatedly reviewed online, and no one is mincing words about it being one of the coolest places in Austin. They are calling this spot, upscale and go as far as to say, they hit the Mocktail trend on the nose!

We are believers, as the online reviewers, tell you what they think whether you want to know or not. Check it out Mock Stars!

THE MOCKTAIL: The No. 9 Dream

The No. 9 Dream blends apricot preserves, ginger, citrus, Chinese five spice, and shiso. Sounds intoxicating addictive and it is zero proof; something like a *love potion, #9* perhaps?

El Naranjo, 85 Rainey Street, Austin, Texas (512-474-2776)

THE MOCKTAIL: Fresca including horchata

THE MOCKTAIL: Hibiscus-based tea Agua de Jamaica

CANADA ZERO PROOF

A couple of the recipes are from *Deflate the Elephant*, which you can find online. I just stepped up, to the bar and made a few of these at home, and thought they were excellent. Sometimes, it's hard to find the particular bitters they reference, so I improvised. Also, it might be of import to know that one litre equals 33.8140227 ounces. Use your phone app to convert if you are not a math wizard and need the conversion done for you. I think these are going to float your boat. Check it out:

THE MOCKTAIL: Mouthwatering Mimosa

1-litre of your favourite grapefruit juice
1-cup orange juice
1-litre club soda or sparkling mineral water- I use club soda in mine
3-5 drops of grapefruit bitters or citrus bitters [drops means drops]
2 blood oranges grapefruits – beautiful these really jazz up the drink!

You will serve your mouthwatering mimosa in a champagne flute, for nothing else will do.

I actually enjoy my Zoejito as I have bragged about, it without the slightest hesitation repeatedly here; but I have to give Deflate the Elephant their due. This is a very fun take on the Mojito.

THE MOCKTAIL: Pomegranate Mojito

4 lime wedges
1 tbsp. superfine sugar
6-8 mint leaves
3 oz. pomegranate juice
club soda
mint sprig
1-cup ice

SOUTH OF THE BORDER

Our own Bev brought these back to us from Mexico. "I now do a lot of work in Mexico and other Latin countries. I used to make my professional business trips to Mexico as if I was a tourist, just there to party my brains out day and night, which of course, I did. Now I make my professional trips, well, professionally. I have figured out the Mock scene quite nicely. All the zing no sting, here are some of my favorites from the W in Mexico City!" Salud, Bev

W Mexico City, Campos Eliseos, 252, 11560 Mexico City, Mexico +525591381800

Mocktail Refresh Water

Watermelon, mint, Perrier (sparkling water), mint and hint of raw sugar

Pepinator/Cucumber Water

Cucumber, lemon and Perrier (hint of jalapeño if desired) for garnish

Cuban Raspberry

Apple juice, raspberries, mint, lime and Perrier

Horchata with a twist (Bev's own recipe)

Horchata and pecans on top for garnish
Mix with water, Almond Milk or Coconut Milk
Add a shot of coffee if you need an extra late night boost!

Mango-on-Mango

Mango, vanilla, ginger, and milk; it's a mango tango in your mouth!

Coconut Water Refresher

Raw coconut water with fresh coconut chunks

POST SCRIPT

From the onset, Bev has been an insider on the making of *Party like a Mock Star!* I invited her to share her story for the book, and she jumped in and gave us the unabridged version. She is walking her talk now, doing her work. At some point down the road, Bev will get involved with our *Party Like a Mock Star* Mocktail Party videos and you will all come to adore her too! Thank you, Bev!

Introducing Beverly

Bev is an amazingly brilliant and talented young lady. Here is her story, retold by Zoe Robinette

Frankly, my dad was a drunk. He bounced out of my life when I was a little girl and never looked back. I learned from him that I wasn't worth his time, his effort or his love. I looked for him my whole youth. I found him repeatedly in the one-night stands, the dudes I wound up falling into the sack with drunk and stoned out of my mind. I truly was crazy with grief over my father even if I didn't get that at the time and I lied incessantly to my church going, mother. It really was a yellow stained road, peeing in the bed, in the street, out of control and out of my mind. I wasted about a decade of my life.

I thought of myself as one of the misfit toys like in that kid's movie. I was the windup-party-girl-doll, who wore the party mask. The Wind me up, put a drink in my hand and I partied until I tipped over and you put me back on the shelf. I became that windup party doll that was stuck in the land of the misfit toys.

At one point, I was such an intoxicated little mess that I wished my college friends, those that I had left would just put me in a stroller and push me from party to party. I tried so hard to fit in that I stuck out even amongst the biggest of the partiers. The misfit-toy-windup version of a young lady wearing the party girl mask that was me and I was never without my mask. I have been drunk, intoxicated and otherwise fucked up in several different countries, and many different states. The places are as different as can be, some of the finest places on the planet and some not. Some of the dudes I was with were just a better class of loser. The places were different, but my stories were the same. Passed out little party girl misfit toy doll. Someone would always get me dressed again and put me into bed, or into a car and off I went on another wild adventure. I didn't remember a lot of those stories, which is good; and I do remember a lot of the stories, which is equally good, and the only thing that saved me. Remembering what I was doing to that little misfit toy doll who lived inside of me literally kept me alive.

Happy Birthday sweet sixteen, not so sure about sweet, but by the time my twenty-first birthday rolled around I already had 3 fake IDs that I carried in my purse at all times. Have fake ID will party; got me tossed into jail. That was not an easy night, I remember trying to pump up in the clink just in case I had to take on some harden criminal chick who was jailed in there with me. I forget how it all ended.

I spent most of my twenties and into my 30s in front of a toilet bowl puking my guts out and hungover on my sofa the next Sunday morning. I called those my wonder years. I wondered if that was how I was going to live the rest of my life praying to the toilet and on Sunday watching my mother pray for my salvation.

I just switched one addiction for another, booze for drugs, sex for danger, one club for another, one party store for another, until I was down to the bottom and it started to look like up. I did it all intoxicated, fucked up, messed up and those times are too unreal to me now to be real. But I did those things, drove drunk, smacked into cars, hit people in the face, and got naked most of the time. Getting naked was high on my list of misfit toy party girl behavior.

I cannot say I regret my past. I don't. I just learned that the trauma, grief, abandonment, and coping with a life not make in heaven were too much for me to handle. Some of the antics would make great girls go wild movie, in fact, I think there are a few videos out there on the Miss Fit label. All I know is that I had to continue to wear the mask because I had to face people after every messed up episode of the Miss Fit Does Joey Movie.

I finally got to the point that I understood this was my real life. That I wasn't a misfit windup party doll. I wasn't born a party girl. I was born a girl who needed love, protection, and guidance. None of it added up for me. I got tough and chose my own road. That path was leading me nowhere fast. I had to look at myself in the mirror. Actually, look at me. I had always detested looking at myself in the mirror. The truth was shattering. I hid from myself, but I didn't hide the real me from anyone around me. Friends and jobs were falling away. The fun party-girl-mask was starting to get worn and tattered. I was getting extremely worn and tattered and I was still in the best years of my life. What best years?

I can laugh at some of my bizarre behavior now because I lived. None of us died from our close to death experiences in those years, but those years weren't my best. The best is yet to come. I am doing my program. And, I am also Mocking my way back to my strength and beauty. So now girls, instead of taking off my clothes in a drunken stupor I remove my mask and get as real as I can be. I am learning how to be. I am learning how to be me. I am learning how to wind myself up with a healthy dose of exercise, reading, and dancing without the mask. OMG, I feel vulnerable. Feeling vulnerable is the most frightening thing I know. I am doing my best to face the fears, stay real and just fake drink. That's the only thing I fake these days, drinking.

I am grateful to have found a way to really be me, and continue to party and have fun. I am also super glad to be a part of this Mocktail adventure. There is definitely more to come on this story, so stay tuned and Mock On!

While my own experiences may not have been as dramatic as my girl Bev's, I certainly had my moments as a wild child.

Moreover, the further I got away from being that way via Mocking, the more I loved it and I loved myself too. Before I knew it, I was taking on each new event as another challenge to perfect my Mocking and I have shared a few of those experiences with you.

This is an exciting time and fulfills my mission of empowering women to be authentic and to live a truly happy life. I hope you join us for more Mock Star adventures.

TAPPING INTO THE BEST OF THE BEST

"And we've only just begun" - The Carpenters

We will be clubbing at hottest spots in the country, where the best mixologists on the planet, will be hosting our Party Like a Mock Star video segments.

Mock Star Episode at BOA with our host mixologist Tara Shadzi

For one of our first live Mock Star video episodes, we will be doing a segment on the Sunset Strip at the famous, BOA Steak House.

BOA is a favorite of mine and located at 9200 Sunset Blvd. West Hollywood, CA. Los Angeles.

Pretty people, gorgeous Sunset Strip setting, BOA, is sleek and sexy as the West Hollywood diners who gather at it; never disappoints, BOA is truly fabulous!

We will be treated to a savory Mocktail, at the hand of the infamous Miss Mixologist, Tara Shadzi one of the best in the business.

Tara Shadzi has been mixing drinks for nearly ten years and has never looked back.

Training with acclaimed bar chefs such as Tony Abou-Ganim (Iron Chef), Dale DeGroff (Rainbow Room, NYC), and John Lermayer (The Florida Room, Miami) inspired Tara to master the craft of the cocktail.

In 2009, Tara won the Damrak Gin LA cocktail competition for her Rosemary, Sauvignon Blanc, Ouzo, lemon, and gin martini.

Judged by LA Times Food critics, Tara was sent to Amsterdam to attend the Bols Bartending Academy.

She was featured in Esquire's "Bartender Wisdom" and an AP article "Oscar Inspired cocktails" as a mixologist with her bourbon, rose, and elderflower confection.

Last year, she was a presenter at "Taste of Beverly Hills" on stage with Joe Brooke (Absolut's America's best bartender.)

She also has her own webisode called MissMixologist.tv and was plugged in a Mondrian, "Back of House" article.

Tara is passionate about wine and is a 2nd level Sommelier, certified through the International Sommelier Guild.

She has created original recipes for several establishments as she continues to mix cocktails at celebrity hot spot BOA Steakhouse in West Hollywood, and world renowned Skybar at the Mondrian Hotel.

Mocktail Party ™ at the famous Riot House Restaurant and Bar at The Andaz

The Andaz on the famous Sunset Strip will host a Mocktail Party™ doing it up with fabulous Mocktails for our *Party Like a Mock Star* episodes!

THE FAMOUS RIOT HOUSE BAR

The Riot House Bar!

Once a hangout for hard-partying rockers of the 70's, Riot House Bar offers a vibrant space and engaging atmosphere for sipping, relaxing and flirting on Sunset Boulevard.

Indulge in an after-meeting Mocktail or the laid-back happy hour at Riot House Bar.

The hip rooftop bar in Los Angeles features signature Mocktails and delectable bites that come straight out of the Riot House kitchen.

Sip California signature drinks while taking in spectacular views of the Sunset Strip.

The refreshingly relaxed West Hollywood bar also serves excellent vodkas, bourbons, tequilas, and any other spirit you desire, for those in your crowd who are into libations.

The Riot House mixologists serve up handcrafted classic and modern cocktails and delightful Mocktails when you are taking a break and giving your system a re-boot!

Here is one of The Riot House drinks I call The Mock Star Relief:

THE MOCKTAIL: Virgin Aloe from the Other Side
- 1.5 oz. The House secret ingredient
- 3/4 oz. Aloe Vera
- ½ oz. Lime
- ½ oz. Ginger Syrup
- 2 Slices Cucumber
- Club Soda

Muddle cucumber and then add all ingredients except club soda. Shake and strain into glass.

Top with Soda.

Garnish: Aloe Leaf or Cucumber Wedge

Stemware: Copper Mug or Tall Rocks

Look for our *Party Like a Mock Star* video episodes and for our live *Party Like a Mock Star* actual Mocktail Party™ Happy Hours!

Party Like a Mock Star is delighted to introduce our premiere sponsor:

Mocktails Brand® - Alcohol-Free Cocktails

Mocktails Brand® is the first premium brand of ready to drink, alcohol-free (0.0%) cocktail.

It is a fun alternative - enjoy at every occasion, it's the new way to party!™

To learn more about our sponsor **Mocktails Brand®** and locations where you may purchase their delicious, *"Pregnant Mother Approved®; made with real fruit juices, exotic and natural flavors, and pure cane sugar, gluten-free and non-GMO Mocktails Brand® alcohol-free cocktails"* visit them online at www.mocktails.com

Finally, our Mocktail Party scene is coming to you! Join *Party Like a Mock Star* and our sponsor, Mocktails Brand®, at our live Mocktail Party™ Happy Hours!

What we will be serving up? The fabulous Mocktail Brand® healthy alcohol-free cocktails of course!!

- Karma Sucra Cosmopolitan
- The Vida Loca Margarita
- Sevilla Red Sangria
- Scottish Lemonade Whiskey Sour

For more information: www.mockstar.tv, and in the meantime, Mock On!

ABOUT THE AUTHOR:

Zoe Robinette cultivated her joy for performance, theatrics and the art of the tall tale early in life in the middle of the Michigan mitten; her endeavors as a creative writer temporarily upended by her zest for dance, choreography, and health physiology. Zoe earned a couple of master's degrees in dance fitness and health at Central Michigan University [CMU], all while raising two beautiful children. After earning her degrees, Zoe coordinated CMU's first health fitness program and taught dance classes until she dropped. Then she lost her mind and stumbled into hospital administration, where the art of drinking cocktails became a near necessary skill to endure the endless hours of schmoozing and elbow rubbing. Zoe still continues to dance and will until she keels over but she has returned to her first love, writing.

Zoe is a woman who wears many hats (seriously, she has a lot of hats). Not only is she a writer but she also has a panache for jump-starting medical practices and she enjoys consulting. Zoe lives, works, and plays in Los Angeles where she is engaged in public relations functions, networking and social soireés that give her plenty of inspiration for her "Mock Tales." If she's not working on her stories you can find her reading, fantasizing about being listed on Forbes most influential women of the Century, planting pretty flowers, working with blue chip corporations or indulging in her unhealthy addiction to chocolate and Mock Cosmopolitans.

Manor House
www.manor-house.biz
Visit: www.mockstar.tv

Manor House
www.manor-house.biz
Visit: www.mockstar.tv

CPSIA information can be obtained
at www.ICGtesting.com
Printed in the USA
LVHW082056250619
622140LV00033B/470/P